"*Your Children Should Know* is passionate, lucid, skillful, respectful and a major addition to a field too often crowded with second-rate information."

—Sandra Butler,
author of *Conspiracy of Silence:
The Trauma of Incest*

"This book offers counselling advice, self-defense encouragement, and sympathy with down-to-earth simplicity. *Your Children Should Know* is one of the best sources of understanding and coping."

—Detective Ellen King,
Sex Crimes Unit,
New York City Police Department

"*Your Children Should Know* should be on the shelf of every public library and in everyone's home."

—A. Nicholas Groth, Ph.D.,
author of *Men Who Rape*

"A must for anyone who has ever loved a child."

—Susan Gershatter Smith, CSW,
former director of
Manhattan Girls Club

Your Children Should Know

Personal-Safety Strategies For Parents To Teach Their Children

by Flora Colao and Tamar Hosansky

PERENNIAL LIBRARY

Harper & Row, Publishers
New York, Cambridge, Philadelphia, San Francisco
London, Mexico City, São Paulo, Singapore, Sydney

We dedicate this book to Debbie,
whom we never knew.
Your spirit prevails in your friends.
They have taught us how to
help other children survive.

———

A hardcover edition of this book was originally published in 1983 by
The Bobbs-Merrill Company, Inc. It is here reprinted by arrange-
ment with The Bobbs-Merrill Company, Inc.

First PERENNIAL LIBRARY edition published 1987.

———

Library of Congress Cataloging-in-Publication Data

Colao, Flora.
  Your children should know.

  Reprint. Originally published: Indianapolis:
Bobbs-Merrill, 1983.
  Includes index.
  1. Child molesting—Prevention. 2. Child
abuse—Prevention. I. Hosansky, Tamar. II. Title.
HQ71.C69 1987   362.7′1   86-46215
ISBN 0-06-097104-5 (pbk.)

———

87 88 89 90 91 MPC 10 9 8 7 6 5 4 3 2 1

Contents

ON GUARD! A photographic guide to self-defense for young people follows page 100.

Foreword

Flora Colao:

"I was breastfeeding my daughter the first time she tried to bite. Following the advice of all the experts, I firmly told her no and took my breast away. She didn't try biting again until after she was weaned. She was slightly over a year old. Again, I firmly told her no. I added that biting was wrong and uncivilized (I actually used that word as it seemed to get her attention). I repeated the process when she started hitting. Within a few weeks she neither bit nor hit anyone. I had succeeded! I was a good mother. My child was going to grow up to be a peaceful, loving person, resolving conflicts in a non-violent way. I was so proud, especially when other mothers told me that she seemed like such a good child.

"One day when she was playing in the sandbox with several other children, she picked up another child's shovel. He responded by biting her. She raised her hand to hit him and stopped herself. Then she burst into tears. Her look of anger and betrayal was not directed at the child who bit her. It was directed at me. I had left her defenseless and unprotected. Despite my good intentions, instead of creating a peaceful, loving person I was creating a perfect victim with no outlet for her anger. It was a frightening insight. I had no idea how to begin to undo the damage I had already done. There were no experts to consult, no books to read.

"I began researching the problem of sexual assault in 1975 while working on my master's degree in social work. I developed and implemented the St. Vincent's Hospital Rape Crisis Program in 1976. My first exposure to working with children around the issue of sexual assault was counselling children who had been present when their mothers had been assaulted. Later, I started receiving referrals of children who had been victimized themselves. I noticed certain patterns in what children were saying to me about their understanding of what happened and why it happened, as well as what they were saying to me and not saying to their parents and other care providers. I also became aware of patterns of attack against children. In addition, I found that all of the children developed some kind of physical symptoms, ranging from pains to nausea to shaking to heart pounding.

"I was identifying many issues and amassing quite a bit of information and soon recognized that these children needed both physical and emotional outlets in order to recover from sexual assault. This crystallized for me when I was working with a ten-year-old girl who had been molested. Every time she came to my office she would stamp her feet. When I asked her about it, she told me that she liked to pretend that the floor was her attacker's face. I knew at that point that I had to find a place where children could be allowed to release their physical as well as emotional feelings, and I consulted SAFE."

Tamar Hosansky:

"I started studying the martial arts in 1974. I began with an eight-week self-defense course and found that I didn't want to stop. I continued with formal karate and earned a black belt. I have been studying ever since. I and several of my fellow students began teaching in various health clubs and martial arts schools. We noticed that these programs were not attracting the people most fearful of crime nor those most likely to be victimized: senior citizens, children, women, and the disabled. We also felt that the techniques that were being taught were not practical defenses against the types of attack that were most common, nor were they easily mastered. In addition, I found that my own training had given me little outlet for the emotional responses I had while learning how to defend myself and how to fight. At that time, few martial arts programs addressed the conditioning that stops people from defending themselves in the first place: fear of hurting someone, fear of being killed, fear of panicking. Most of the crime-prevention literature available consisted of a series of don'ts and shouldn't dos that were not practical. Pamela McDonnell and I started the Safety and Fitness Exchange (SAFE) as an alternative to traditional crime prevention and martial arts programs.

"SAFE began in 1979 as a consulting firm. We conducted seminars nationally for corporations, associations, schools, and community organizations. We designed positive, upbeat programs, tailoring safety plans to the needs of the participants. In 1980 we expanded, opening a self-defense school with ongoing classes. Soon after the school opened, we collaborated with Flora to begin the children's program.

"Our first students were Flora's clients, about ten children, most of whom had been sexually assaulted. We knew that recovering from sexual assault meant giving the children control over their bodies and their environment. The classes were controlled by the children; the space for that hour was theirs. They created games, hit targets, punched and yelled. We put on boxing gloves and sparred with them. We let them talk about their feelings and draw pictures. Soon we began to notice that many of the children's physical symptoms diminished. In its first year the program was ever-changing as we continued to experiment and take our leads from the children. Eventually, a coherent program with an identifiable structure and philosophy emerged.

"As other children joined and their parents watched, we were asked how we taught children and how other parents and teachers could help children be safer. We began to get press coverage, which resulted in our receiving requests for information from all over the country. One article stated that we had a pamphlet on teaching children personal safety. We received hundreds of requests for it. Frantically, we wrote a pamphlet. On the pamphlet we wrote, 'Excerpted from a forthcoming book.' At that time, the idea of writing a book on our work with children was a dream. We began receiving requests for the book. We realized that in order to meet the growing demand for the information, we had to write a book. Since then, the program has grown to proportions far beyond what we originally envisioned. People always ask us how we do it. All I can think of when people ask are those first classes, with ten sexual assault victims, and how many of our friends and colleagues didn't understand what we were doing. All I can think of as an answer is to thank those children, because they taught us everything we know."

Acknowledgments

We wish to individually acknowledge the following:

From Tamar Hosansky:

My grandparents, for a legacy of survival.
My parents, for long-standing faith in my success.
My brother David, the first child I ever loved.
Susan, for love unconditional and freedom unlimited.
Christopher, for the chance to be a child.
Jenny, for constant encouragement.
Seda, Pat, Pam, and Stevie, for a home by a lake to write in, flowers by my typewriter, horseback rides, and smiles from babies.
All my martial arts instructors for teaching me that fear is a challenge, not an obstacle.
Kathy, who believed me first.

From Flora Colao:

Michael, for love, support, and hugs that have constantly sustained me through my work and this book.
Nicole, for helping me rediscover magic and the joys of childhood.
My grandparents, for a sense of history; and in particular, Grandma Lucy who was the first to teach me that abused children can grow to become caring and loving adults.

My parents, for strength and pride.

My sister Rita, for nurturance for as long as I can remember.

My brothers, Anthony, John, and Gino, for teaching me how to fight.

Ellen Halloran, for friendship and for designing my necklace, the symbol of strength I always wear.

Nęlia Sellers, for ten years of support and encouragement.

Jean Millar, for doing her work so well, which enabled me to do mine.

Dr. Philip W. Brickner, for the opportunity to begin.

The staff of the Department of Community Medicine, for managing with my daughter and her toys in the office.

The volunteers of the Rape Crisis Program and NYWAR, for carrying much of the load.

Elizabeth Healy and Ellen Quirke, for wisdom that guided me in much of my work.

Danny Beaudoin, for delightful breakfasts and good chuckles.

Together, we gratefully acknowledge:

Pam McDonnell, for believing in us before she even understood what we were doing.

Risa Breckman, for dinners, ice cream, and late-night phone calls.

Sandra Elkin, for enthusiasm and hard work.

Barbara Lagowski, for saying, "It's fabulous, fabulous, fabulous!"

The Goldstock/Tower family, for allowing disruption of their lives at all hours so we could use their word processor.

Anne Sparks, for her smiles.

Katherine Brady, for taking on the obstacle course in our children's class.

Gino Colao, for patience and pictures.

Christopher Alexander, for posing in our technique shots.

Ellie Grossman, for telling the country we had a pamphlet before we had one.

Jane Cotton, for a peaceful house to write in.

Our local Chinese restaurant and ice cream parlor, for delivery at odd hours.

All the children in our programs, for teaching us.

And finally, each other, for efforts that go far beyond collaboration.

Introduction to the Perennial Library Edition

When we first wrote *Your Children Should Know*, we wanted people to face the reality of child abuse. We planned to present concrete positive alternatives based on our specific experience with children. We wanted to help parents, teachers, and other professionals give children non-alarmist practical information and training so they could learn to effectively protect themselves. Our primary goal was to empower children without frightening them.

Over the past few years, the problem of crimes against children has received national recognition. Concerned parents want to protect their children but don't want to make them distrustful or paranoid. And many childcare professionals and educators are now mandated to teach abuse prevention and to report suspected incidences of abuse. Yet few adults feel secure about their own self-defense capabilities. Consequently, adults are in the position of trying to teach children strategies they themselves are not confident using. In addition, adults are often so frightened and uncomfortable discussing crime with children that they present vaguely defined dangers and oversimplified solutions.

In order to have effective prevention and aftercare programs, it is crucial to listen to children, and to learn from their behaviors and gestures. By following this principle, you can apply the concepts and information we share in this book to situations in your children's lives. In our work with thousands of children across the country, we have heard their current concerns:

"They always tell you to say, 'No,' but grownups
don't listen when you say no, even if you yell it."

Children need to be given a variety of options. To tell
them to say no without giving them a way to handle the
adult who refuses to listen leaves them still vulnerable. Children are painfully aware from experience that adults seldom
listen to them. Children don't expect adults to respect their
'No.'' Consequently, children need to have an opportunity
to practice saying no and to have that no respected before
we can expect them to be able to say no in an abusive
situation.

"I know what sexual abuse is; that's when someone
touches the bad parts of your body"

We are gravely concerned that we may have a generation
of children growing up believing that parts of their body are
bad. Because of adults' discomfort with sexuality issues,
they have created euphemisms to teach children about sexual assault. Children are literal beings. They need clear,
concrete, and accurate information about what sexual abuse
is. They also need positive information about sex and sexuality. In order to define sexual abuse, we must tell children
the correct names for their body parts and distinguish sexual
abuse from sexuality.

"They say don't let anyone touch you in a bad way,
but then they hit you."

From a child's perspective, getting smacked, being
dragged down the street when they're walking too slowly,
having a teacher push them into a seat, etc., are 'bad'
touches. Having their genitals fondled by a molester may
not feel like a bad touch to a child. This is often upsetting
and confusing for children. Unfortunately, in this culture,
children do not have the right to simply say no to touches
they define as bad. They only have the right to say no to
touches that are defined as illegal. It is no wonder that children are confused and frightened by the proliferation of information about child abuse.

"Every morning at breakfast I see the faces of missing
children on the milk carton. I know this sounds silly,
but I feel as though I'm drinking blood."

In their efforts toward helping to remedy the problem of abduction, few adults take into account the devastating emotional effect this has had on children. Our children are constantly confronted with the problem without being able to express their fears or concerns. When they ask for solutions, they are still being told, 'Don't talk to strangers,' which is perhaps the most impractical advice given to children. In addition to needing strategies that they themselves can implement, it is imperative to tell children of the situations when other children have successfully averted danger.

"I thought that, after I told, I was going to that pretty place for children that I saw on the TV movie. But they sent me to a shelter. I was all alone."

Unfortunately, child sexual abuse victims may have a difficult time even when they are brave enough to report the abuse. Many adults present children with a neat package of what will happen if they report. Children can be helped, but they must have knowledgeable adults willing to advocate on their behalf. It is also crucial that they be told the truth about what will happen and what their options are, or they will feel betrayed by the helpers as well as the abusers. Children can be helped by a community that cares, even when the situations are not optimal.

Parents and teachers are well aware of the many programs and products on the market that attempt to deal with the public's ever-growing demand for information on safety. Unfortunately, few of these programs and products take the child's perspective into account (see "Afterword: How to Evaluate Children's Safety Programs"). *Your Children Should Know* was written with a child's-eye view of the adult-controlled world. Using children's natural imaginativeness, versatility, and capabilities, we devised tactics for recognizing and preventing dangerous situations.

Based on our experience with children who have been abused, we discovered how to help them heal from traumatic situations and regain their confidence and self-esteem. We've also learned that parents and others can make a difference. Success stories abound. Children can triumph.

They can learn to protect themselves and they can heal when abuse occurs.

> "My son burst into tears after the news story of the child who was kidnapped. I was glad I had read the book. Instead of saying, 'Don't worry, honey,' I was able to address his fears realistically and give him ideas of what to do to prevent it from happening to him."

> "My daughter told me that my husband had been molesting her. I didn't know what to do. I went to the library and asked for a book on child abuse. They gave me *Your Children Should Know* and I opened to the chapter "What to Do if It Happens." I was glad that you gave step-by-step information that I could use even when I was that upset."

> "I was in the park with my four-year-old daughter and my new baby. My daughter was behind me so I didn't see when that woman picked her up. I heard my daughter scream, 'I want to go back to Mommy!' I turned around to see the woman heading toward the exit. I yelled at my daughter to kick hard and screamed instructions to get the other mothers mobilized. My daughter was saved thanks to what we learned from the book."

> "This is the best. It is the only one that has children telling their own stories. It has both prevention and aftercare. Each time I read it I learn something new. It's been invaluable in my work."

We believe in children's strength and intelligence. We have learned much from the children we've worked with. We want to pass on what we have learned. Our goal is to teach parents and professionals how to help create an inner feeling of safety in children. This will encourage the growth of their innate strength and intelligence and have far-reaching effects throughout their lives.

1

Why Your Children Should Know

My nine-year-old son came home and told me that he had been in the park riding his bicycle when a teenager came up to him and began a conversation. My son was flattered that an older boy was paying attention to him. They talked for quite a while and became very friendly. Then the teenager said that his father was going to buy him a bicycle and he wasn't sure what kind he wanted. He asked my son if he could try his bicycle and ride it to the nearby lamppost and back. My son agreed. The teenager got on the bicycle and rode away with it. My son felt like a fool. Later he said to me, "Ma, you always told me about strangers, but you never told me about things like that. He was not a stranger. He had become a friend."—I didn't know what to say.

Children are taught from an early age that there are dangers in the world. They are told not to touch electrical outlets; they are taken on fire drills; they are taught to watch for cars on the street; how to handle scissors and other sharp objects. These are simple lessons for parents to teach—the dangers are clear and the prevention is clear.

Children are also warned of other dangers. They are told not to talk to strangers, not to accept candy, gifts, or rides from people they don't know, not to play in the schoolyard alone, and countless other "shouldn't dos." They are seldom told precisely *what* they are supposed to be wary of in these situations, and rarely is the ominous "stranger" defined for them. Is it a man? A woman? Can children be strangers? What will

1

strangers do if one talks to them? Or accepts candy? What children are most apt to learn from hinted, veiled warnings is fear. And armed only with murky information about undefined threats to their well-being, it is no wonder that children's nightmares generally involve scary strangers or unknown beings.

If we adults stop to think about what we are warning our children against, we become nervous, upset, guilty, and angry. *It* is not something we want to talk about. We hope that our vague warnings will be sufficient to keep our children frightened away from the unspeakable. The fact is, *it* has become a problem of staggering dimensions. Though only the tip of the iceberg has emerged, we find that sexual assault and abuse of children is a national epidemic. One in four girls is sexually assaulted before she reaches her eighteenth birthday, and recent evidence indicates that boys may be at equal risk. Experts agree that incest occurs in approximately one in ten families. Add to those startling figures all the children who are siblings or close friends of those who are victimized, all the children who never tell anyone that they have been abused, and all the children whose mothers are assaulted, and it amounts to one in two children directly or indirectly affected by sexual assault. But the problem is again compounded by perhaps the most upsetting finding—it is not the stranger who is most likely to harm our children; in 85 percent of the cases a child is sexually assaulted by someone s/he knows and trusts.

Few professionals have been taught how to cope with or successfully intervene in cases of child sexual abuse. Some psychiatrists, social workers, and medical personnel, schooled in classic psychoanalytic training have been taught that children fantasize sexual abuse. Thus, children have frequently been told that the incidents of abuse they report are imagined or outright lies. Even when the child is believed, it is often assumed that s/he provoked the act in some way. ("These children are seductive.") Some put the onus on the parents. ("What did you expect, she was in the park by herself?") In situations where the child is believed and not blamed for the assault, professionals will often give parents advice such as, "Don't talk about it and he'll forget what happened" or, "Pretend nothing happened; she seems fine."

Parents who are concerned about the issue *before* anything happens to their child and seek professional advice are often told that to discuss sexual assault will only scare their children, give them frightening notions about sexuality, or make them paranoid and distrustful. Even when confronted with blatant medical evidence, parents and professionals alike will deny the possibility that a sexual assault has occurred, again escaping the issue. In addition, because of the lack of professional training in this area, many care providers are reluctant to take on abused juvenile clients because they feel inadequate to provide appropriate care.

As this issue gathers public attention, adults are coming forward in large numbers to report incidents of sexual abuse from their childhoods. They confirm that these incidents have caused severe problems, many of which carried over well into adulthood. They also report that the most devastating effects were often caused by people's responses to them when they tried to get help. Many adults acknowledge that as children they never told anyone of the incident; that the sexual assault was a burden they carried alone.

Few people understand how a child can be sexually assaulted and not tell anyone. Some of the reasons why a child will not seek help when s/he is suffering abuse may be: (1) the child is physically, financially, or emotionally dependent on the abuser; (2) the abuser has threatened the child's safety or that of the family ("If you tell, I'll kill your mother."); (3) the child blames himself for what happened (Abusers often feed into this: "I did this to you because you are bad."); (4) the child has been taught that the good are rewarded and the bad are punished and therefore assumes responsibility for the assault ("This happened to me because I went out when I wasn't supposed to."); (5) the child fears that no one will believe her, either because the abuser is a known and trusted adult ("How can you say such a thing about your grandfather?") or because they have no proof ("What do you mean he hurt you, there's nothing wrong with you."); (6) the child has been given the message that sexual issues are never discussed; (7) the child does not have words to explain what happened ("Uncle Joe is always bothering me."), and the adults in the child's environment aren't able to pick up on what the child means; (8) the child totally blocks the incident from his or her memory, due to the trauma of the assault.

We do not know how many children today are suffering in silence with no one to turn to or no words to describe what has happened to them. Our ignorance of the scope of the problem will continue until we have access to accurate information about prevention of abuse as well as training adequate to the handling of cases after abuse has occurred.

In developing our work with children, we found that prevention and aftercare are inseparable. As we gave children prevention information, they often disclosed incidents of abuse that had already occurred or that they were currently coping with. When counseling children and their families after an assault, many requested safety strategies and prevention information. Many felt it was the only way they could feel safe and look positively toward the future. We found that combining prevention and aftercare was the most effective way of addressing the problem.

Imparting information in a way that children could grasp and use meant learning how to view the world from a child's perspective. In addition, we had to challenge not only the traditional ways in which children are taught about personal safety but society's view of childhood and childrearing as well. We had to set aside our preconceived ideas and open ourselves to learning from children. The children we work with taught us that children know much more than we had previously thought possible, that they learn in many ways, that each thing they learn carries over to other aspects of their lives, and that often problems that are upsetting and frightening for adults to talk about are everyday realities for children.

We discovered that by not limiting our expectations of children's potential, their growth could far exceed anything we imagined possible. We learned to put ourselves in the position of facilitators and were privileged to see the transformation of children's lives. Rather than becoming frightened or paranoid, children were exhilarated by their new knowledge. Boys and girls of all ages learned to work together cooperatively and problem-solve in many areas.

Initially, many children expected to have a difficult time learning self-defense. They viewed themselves as weak or clumsy or simply incapable of learning. Once in an environment where the adults perceived them to be strong and capable, however, the children mastered all the skills quickly. After a few classes they had learned how to successfully break out of holds, get help when in danger, and develop a variety of effective avoidance strategies in a minimum of time. Contrary to some parental and professional concerns that children would misuse their newly acquired physical skills and become aggressive or violent, we found that children learned to channel their strength and skills appropriately. They confidently used assertiveness techniques to deal with the school bully or similar situations and resorted to physical techniques only when it was the safest option.

Given the opportunity to verbalize their fears and discuss their problems with other children, many developed an increased self-esteem which permeated all aspects of their lives. For some, nightmares turned around—in their dreams, they chased the monster away and became Superman or Wonder Woman. Children who were made fun of for being chubby or slow learners found that all the other children had something that they were also teased about. Together, they developed positive ways of handling teasing.

As we developed our work with children, we found that a lot of feelings were aroused in us. We found ourselves looking back at our own childhoods and reexamining our feelings about children. We had to put aside legal definitions of sexual assault, because they did not deal with the scope of the problems children face. We also had to ignore or question much of the professional, medical, and psychological literature because it did not realistically address the issues. We found ourselves in a continuous process of re-thinking societal attitudes about children.

Children are the most vulnerable members of our society, yet they are the last to be given any information about how to protect themselves. Through our work we have developed non-alarmist and practical ways of transmitting safety information to children, of helping them learn to use their size, speed and environment to their advantage, and of helping them recover if an assault occurs.

In our work, we see many adults facing uncomfortable feelings and memories. We fully expect that this book will arouse the full range of emotions. We also expect that this book will take you on a path of rediscovering childhood. Seeing the world through the eyes of a child is an experience that even those intimately involved with children seldom allow themselves to have. This book is written for anyone who is involved with children on any level. It will help you take a look at the world from their perspective, which is sometimes frightening and oftentimes joyful. It will also clarify the ways to communicate personal safety information to children as well as how to help children recover from an assault on themselves or someone they love.

We have written this book for yesterday's children, with the hope of relieving their burden and letting them know that they no longer have to carry it alone; for today's children, with the hope of sparing them tomorrow's pain; and for the children of the future, with the hope and conviction that the world will become a safe place to be a child.

2

Children Are Special

When my daughter was four years old, we started increasing her responsibility for keeping her room clean, putting her toys away, and hanging her clothes up. We put up hooks at her level so she could hang things up and taught her how to put clothes on hangers. One day I opened her closet door and discovered a number of the things she was to have hung up on the floor of the closet. When I asked her why she didn't hang up her clothes, she answered, "I did Mommy. I hung them up, but the closet fairies knocked them off the hangers." I asked her to tell me about the closet fairies. She told me that there were red, green, and pink ones, that they had pointy ears, and that the child fairies were always doing bad things like knocking clothes off hangers. She added that the mommy fairies got angry about that and would shake them by their ears when they found out. I remarked, "They're probably going to get a good shaking for knocking down all these clothes." She giggled and we hung up her clothes together. I'm glad I let her tell me about her fairies. It was a lot of fun, it stimulated her imagination, and she ended up hanging her clothes up better after that. Several days later she even admitted that the closet fairies weren't real.

We rarely allow ourselves to experience the world from a child's perspective. For children, in the position of being smaller and weaker than most of the people around them, imagination becomes a way of compensating for feeling powerless. Children create magical explanations for occurrences in their daily lives that they have no control over and for feelings that are overwhelming. Magic allows them to feel omnipotent and provides a way for them to channel their emotions. That's part of the reason why superheroes are such popular role models. Little boys dream of being Superman and little girls dream of being Wonder Woman because vicarious association with those godlike characters enables them to feel that they have control over their lives. Children believe in the incredible because the power wielded by adults seems so magical.

> When my son was two I allowed him to watch only *Sesame Street* or *The Muppet Show* on TV. One day he figured out how to turn on the TV and was shocked that neither program was on. He came over to me and said, "Mommy, you do it, put on Kermit the Frog." I told him that they weren't on now, and he said, "You can do it, just change the channel." I explained that they came on later in the day and he cried and protested, "You just don't want to put it on." I showed him all the channels and that those programs were not on. He was still crying and saying, "You just don't want to put it on." It was exasperating. There was no way of explaining to him that I didn't control when the Muppets were on TV."

Children believe that adults have unlimited power in the world because adults have unlimited power over them.

Not only are children in the position of being physically smaller than most of the people around them, but they are emotionally, financially, psychologically, and physically dependent on adults as well. Every aspect of the child's world is controlled by parents, teachers, bus drivers, religious leaders, store owners, doctors, neighbors, and relatives. They decide when and what a child eats, when and where a child sleeps, what a child wears, where a child attends school and which one and if the child attends at all. Adults define good and bad and teach that if you are good you are rewarded and if you are bad you are punished. In addition, adults control children's access to physical affection as well as children's sense of self and reality.

Every adult was once a child. Unlike other forms of oppression, this one all of us share. Though we perceive our "coming

of age" as a time when we have finally "grown out of" childhood, the experiences we had as children remain with us. Sometimes our contacts with children bring back glimpses of ourselves
as youngsters. Through them we can remember what it's like
to view the world with children's eyes, and we can understand
the monsters that sometimes jump out from the shadows.

When I picked my daughter up at school she seemed
unusually quiet. I asked her how her day had been, and
she said, "Not too good." She then told me how she had
gone into the coatroom to put her mittens in her pocket,
and the door had closed behind her. She tried to open
the door, and she could turn the knob but couldn't get
the door open because it was too heavy. She tried several
times and banged on the door to get the other children's
and her teacher's attention. It was music time; they were
playing instruments and singing, so nobody heard her.
After awhile she just sat down on the floor and cried.
She wasn't missed for the whole music period. She was
discovered by her teacher when the children were getting
their coats on to go outside. I couldn't help but cry when
she told me. I suddenly just felt so helpless as I remembered what it was like to be so small and feel so alone.

As adults we often feel vulnerable and helpless in the world.
To recall how much more vulnerable and helpless we were as
children can become emotionally intolerable. Within each adult
there is a child who has had some experience of powerlessness
and fear. For some of us the memories are of being teased by
a sibling, being bullied at school by older children, or being
pushed out of line at the candy store. For others, there are
memories of more severe instances of powerlessness: being
unable to bring a dead pet back to life, being so afraid of the
dark that we couldn't sleep, being unable to stop an accident
that we knew was about to happen, or being unable to make
our sick parent well.

I was seven years old when we were driving home
from visiting my aunt's house. It had been very cold that
day, and the roads were icy. The car started to skid, and
I knew we were going to skid off the road and hit the
tree. I pushed my foot into the floor, wishing that I was

braking the car. We did hit the tree, but luckily none of us were badly hurt. Whenever I feel powerless now, that is what I remember.

For some of us memories of being powerless consist of remembering the words adults used to describe us and the judgments they made about who we were and what we could do.

When I was ten, our teacher held auditions for the school play, which was a musical. Every child had to sing as part of the audition. My teacher told me that I couldn't sing at all. Every child had to have a part, so she put me in the chorus but told me that I wasn't allowed to sing out loud, that I had to mouth the words. She said that one off-key voice, even in the chorus, could ruin the whole show. I was so embarrassed when one of the kids asked me why I wasn't singing. I felt like a failure. To this day, I won't sing, even when I am alone.

Adults control and define a child's reality. This child believed she couldn't sing because her teacher said she couldn't. It never occurred to her to question or challenge the teacher's judgment. This control of a child's reality is maintained in a variety of ways. Sometimes it is through judgment: "this is a good child, that is a bad child"; "she is a pretty child, she is a plain child"; "he is a graceful child, he is a clumsy child," etc. Few of us realize how such judgments affect a child's sense of self as well as his or her ability to take risks and learn.

I was teaching my eight-year-old self-defense student how to break a board. She tried several times and wasn't able to break the board. Finally I told her that her foot was stronger than the board and that I knew she could break it. She protested and said, "No, I can't." I told her to take a deep breath and remember that her foot was stronger than the board. On the next hit she broke it. Her mother was watching and came over to me and said, "I don't believe it. I would have told her to forget it after several tries because I wouldn't have believed that she could do it."

Sometimes control over children is maintained in very, tangible ways. For example, most children, no matter what their parents' financial status, have little access to money. Whether or not they have any depends on their parents' belief systems in regard to allowances, earning money, and gifts of money.

I was nine years old, and I wanted to surprise my mother with a beautiful necklace I had seen in a store window. I had my own savings account that had fifty dollars in it. Every time I got a gift of money for my, birthday, my mother would deposit it into my account. I was not allowed to take money out of the account unless I explained the reason to her and she signed the withdrawal slip. I was so frustrated because I had my own money to buy her the present and I wasn't going to be able to surprise her because there was no way of getting to it without telling her why.

This child was frustrated that he wasn't able to surprise his mother. Another child in more dire circumstances might have resorted to stealing or other means to get the moncy without his or her parents' knowledge.

For children, adults' control over love, attention, and affection, is just as tangible as their control over the child's access to money, food, and clothing. There are infants who have died from being deprived of physical affection. Touch is as necessary for survival as food and drink. This need and the child's dependency on the fulfillment of this need is part of what makes children so vulnerable. Children want to be loved and touched and cuddled by caring and thoughtful adults. Children give freely of their love and need to have that love returned to them unconditionally. However, love in some settings becomes a bargaining tool—the message, whether spoken or nonverbal is that a child will receive affection only if s/he submits to adult control. ("If you don't do this or that, I won't love you anymore.") Such a message raises the possibility that a child's entire world can be taken away from them at the whim of an angry adult. Used repeatedly, such statements panic children because they come to believe that the very root of their world has begun to crumble.

When I was eight I overheard my parents fighting. My father told my mother that he didn't love her anymore and that he was leaving. My mother screamed at him, "You'll never see your children again." My father stormed out of the house. I cried myself to sleep, upset that he hadn't even bothered to come into my room and say goodbye. I was so sure that I would never see him again.

Once we begin to examine the extent of adults' control over children, we can understand why it is so difficult for us to see the world from a child's perspective. It is also clear, however, that in order to begin to communicate effectively with children, particularly about personal safety, it is necessary to remember this perspective. The following exercises will help you to do this.

LOOKING BACK

Close your eyes and remember a time as a child when you felt powerless. Remember all the aspects of it and what you were thinking at the time. Imagine what you would have liked to be able to do in that situation. Imagine what adult you would have liked to have helped you and what you would have liked them to have done. Think about any difference there might be in your life now had you received help in that situation. This exercise may bring up unexpected reactions, especially if the situation you thought of seemed somewhat incidental initially.

I picked a situation that seemed simple and not that devastating. I remembered a time when my dog got lost. I remembered looking for her for days, calling people and asking anyone and everyone if they had seen her. I remembered how I couldn't believe that my parents weren't more upset and that they continued as if life was normal. I wanted them to drop everything and devote themselves to finding my dog. I felt so betrayed. When I think about it now I realize that I lost a lot of respect for them and never really trusted them again. If they had just acknowledged how devastating it was for me and realized I couldn't just get over it, I don't think I would feel this way now.

LIVING IN THE LAND OF THE GIANTS

This is an exercise that will help you understand a child's physical environment. Sit on the floor and look around the room. How high is your body in relation to furniture, windows, doorknobs and light switches? What can you reach and what can't you reach? If you had to get out of the room how could you do it? What chairs would you be comfortable sitting in? How could you reach things without dropping them or knocking other things over? Do this in every room of the house. Can you turn on faucets? Can you reach glasses to get a drink of water? Can you reach your clothing on hangers? Can you reach food? How high up is the ceiling? What would you change if you could design the house to fit someone your size?

When I did this exercise I suddenly remembered being stuck in an elevator when I was six. I couldn't reach the alarm because it was at the top of the control panel. I screamed and waited until my mother realized I had not come back upstairs. I kept thinking, why don't they put the alarm button on the bottom, so kids could reach it.

For the next two exercises you need another adult with you.

YOU'RE SO CUTE

One adult sits on the floor and the other stands. The standing adult pats the seated adult on the head, pinches his/her cheeks and says, "You're so cute. How old are you? What's your name? Where did you get those beautiful eyes? Give me a smile. Don't be shy," and other comments along that order. After a few minutes, switch places. Discuss your feelings after both of you have gone through the exercise.

At first, I kept laughing, until I realized how much smaller I felt and that I didn't know what the rules were. I didn't know how to make my partner stop. My cheeks were hurting. I felt like screaming, especially when I remembered aunts, uncles, and family friends who did

this to me when I was a child. I suddenly thought that
if I was ugly people wouldn't do this. I didn't want to
be pretty anymore.

When I was pinching his cheeks I realized that I would
never even remotely consider behaving in such a manner
with another adult. I was embarrassed, however, when
I realized that I often pat children on the head, tickle
them, and kiss their cheeks without asking their permis-
sion. I resolved that I would never do this to another
child again.

I DON'T BELIEVE YOU

In this exercise, as in the previous one, one adult sits and the
other stands. The adult who is seated makes a statement that
is absolutely true (what their name is, where they live, the sky
is blue, what day it is, what time it is, etc.). The standing adult
denies these statements. For example: Seated Adult: The sky
is blue. Standing Adult: That's not true. Seated Adult: Yes it
is, the sky is blue. Standing Adult: Come on, you know very
well it isn't. Seated Adult: Look out the window, the sky is
blue. Standing Adult: Why are you always making up stories?
Seated Adult: But just look, the sky is blue. Standing Adult:
If you keep lying, I'll have to punish you.

As in the previous exercise, both adults should have a turn
in both roles.

I can't believe what happened. I told him what time
it was and he said I was wrong. I checked my watch and
repeated the time. When he told me my watch must be
broken, I looked around the room for another clock. I
realized how easy it is to make someone self-doubtful.

These exercises give you a glimpse into the child's world.
It is to be hoped they will also provide an understanding of
how easy it is to control children and the extent of the power
adults have over the lives of children. The next step is to
examine our own feelings about children. In addition to not
having much control in the world, children are not usually
accorded much respect. If we examine our vocabulary, this

becomes clear. For example, expressions such as, "You're acting like a child," "When you grow up, you'll understand," "You do that well—for a child," "What a crybaby!" are all statements that are insulting to children. They reflect a societal view of children that is negative and invalidating.

Many of us have internalized this view, despite the fact that we were all once children. Most of us believe that adults have the right to control children's behavior. We are annoyed with the child we are unable to control. These beliefs affect the way we define morals, standards of behavior, expectations, and judgments in regard to children. We teach children that in order to be good they should follow a set of blanket rules. The very definitions of what constitutes a good child and how a good child behaves are part of the problem when teaching personal safety to children. Good children never lie, are never rude, obey adults, never question authority, keep their voices down, and never hit, bite, or scream. In short, good children are easy to victimize because it would never occur to them to do anything in their own defense, do anything against an adult, or to even question an adult. Many of the personal safety strategies that need to be employed in order to empower children directly conflict with the ways we have been taught to properly raise children. It is important for us to think about, examine, and reevaluate our own attitudes about children and our expectations of their behavior.

Once on a family vacation, I got lost driving back to our motel. I had stopped to look at a map when my five-year-old daughter said, "This is the right road, Daddy. We passed that house before. There's that same little black and white dog." I told her to be quiet as I looked at the map again. Then I flagged down another car and asked directions. When the other driver gave me directions, I realized my daughter had been right. It had never occurred to me that she would be so observant and have such a keen sense of direction and could know where we were when I didn't.

Children are people—people who are physically smaller and who have lived for a shorter period of time than adults. In some circumstances children will know more than we do because of their perspective and associations. In the following chapters we will examine how children's place in society makes them especially vulnerable to sexual assault. We will develop positive ways to protect children and to help them learn to protect themselves. If we allow ourselves to stay in touch with the child's perspective, this experience can be mutually gratifying and beneficial. When we understand and appreciate how special children are, it will also enrich our lives as adults.

3

The Personal Stories

No one ever seemed to understand. I went to so many professionals trying to get a handle on it all. Going to the support group and meeting other women who had been there was my salvation. I finally found people who knew exactly what to say and who could hear me.

The experts on childhood sexual assault are the people who go through it: the children and their loved ones. This chapter is a collection of testimonies from children, parents, and other adults looking back on childhood assaults. We conducted the interviews with people who have been our clients and self-defense students, with friends and friends of friends, as well as friends of students and clients. This is not intended to be a "random sampling"; this material is not data for a researcher. Much of our expertise has been developed from listening to personal stories. Most of the information presented throughout this book is gathered from this listening. We hope these testimonies will also give you insight into the reality of childhood sexual abuse. We feel such statements are far more educational than statistics.

The people interviewed in this chapter range in age from five to fifty-seven. The experiences of sexual abuse described here happened to children aged three to sixteen. Some people were raised in rural areas, some in small towns or suburbs, some in urban areas. They reflect various racial, religious, and social backgrounds. The testimonies are presented anonymously. All details that might compromise anonymity have been deleted.

When we finished conducting the interviews, we had over

fifty hours of tapes. Reams of written material had been given to us. It is our feeling that each story really deserves its own book. We edited them, with great difficulty, to include the points we felt most important for others to know. While we found tremendous commonality in symptoms, reactions, and feelings, we have tried to present what is unique to each story. We did this in order to demonstrate the full spectrum of emotions and experiences connected with childhood sexual assaults. In addition, the people interviewed, as well as others, are quoted throughout the book for the same purpose.

We expect this chapter to elicit a wide range of feelings, including pain, rage, and grief. During the interviews, people found themselves reexperiencing many of the feelings that occurred at the time of the assault. In addition, many found themselves reevaluating different aspects of their experiences. Forgotten pieces were remembered and put into new perspectives. You may also find yourself looking back at your own experiences. We hope that this chapter will break the isolation of those of you who felt, and may still feel, alone. We also hope to give added understanding to those who may never have dealt with such experiences personally.

Of course, what cannot be transferred from interviews into print are the long pauses after our questions, the tears, the trembling, and the anguished expressions of those speaking to us. We think that their courage and strength shines through. We thank all those who agreed to be interviewed for their brave and honest sharing.

ADULTS LOOKING BACK

This section consists of testimonies of men and women looking back on childhood sexual assaults. Some have had total retention of the memory of an assault throughout their childhoods and into their adult years. Others have only recently named the incident as an assault. In some cases there was complete blocking of the experience until adulthood. There are a number who know that "something happened" but who have not as yet recalled the memory. Only one incident was reported to the police. Others were reported to parents. Many went unreported. In all the cases no one received even minimal emotional care. We will let the stories speak for themselves.

R.

I was five years old. I thought it happened because I was Jewish and I was pretty. He said something about what a pretty little Jewish girl I was. I knew even at that age that somehow being Jewish was bad. He waved the knife and said he'd cut my pretty little Jewish face up. I stopped believing in God.

He was my friend's brother. I think he was a soldier home on leave. When he attacked me, I didn't know what he was doing. I felt this sharp pain. I thought he'd stabbed me. I couldn't understand why I was still alive.

I still can't talk. It still feels like there are no words to explain what happened to me. Whenever someone gets angry at me or I'm having a fight with someone, there is a part of me that is still on that roof with a knife at my throat, pinned down. He laughed a lot. He made fun of me a lot. He was so violent and so cold. Even now, teasing feels very violent to me.

I blocked it almost immediately. I split into two people afterwards. I went up to my room and crawled into my bed. I remember the other part of me watching and wanting to hold her, but I couldn't. I told myself I was no good.

He cleaned me up. He told me not to tell anyone. He said he would do the same thing to my mother. I remember once when I was six she went out to buy milk or something. She was delayed getting back because she stopped to talk to someone. When she came back I was hysterical. I thought he'd killed her.

Throughout my adolescence I was depressed. I used to cut myself. I used to put cigarettes out on my arm. I couldn't feel. I was numb. Nobody asked me what was wrong.

Everytime I talk to a man, sleep with a man, relate to a man, it's exhausting. I never feel comfortable. I really want to be able to love a man. He'd have to be able to deal with a lot of pain, a lot of nightmares, a lot of screaming, a lot of tears, and a lot of sex that stops and starts. It's easier to relate to women.

Children need to know specifics about what can happen to them. They have to know what rape is. I think that would have helped me.

Y.

I went home and told my parents. They said, "It's all right, don't worry about it. We'll take care of it. Just forget it." I was really concerned because I was having these sexual feelings and I didn't know what they were. I remember trying to verbalize them to my father. He just said, "Don't worry about it." I remember thinking, What is all this? I had a lot of ambivalence and a lot of guilt. I remember walking to school and feeling different. I knew something significant had happened. I looked at the other children and I knew I was different. I remember feeling guilty about sexual feelings and masturbation after that and thinking the whole thing was wrong and bad. I thought it was some kind of disease. There was so much stimulation. The feelings´ were of enormous ambivalence, of enjoying it, of being terrified, of being anxious at the same time, and being very confused. Talk about control—I was really out of control. He knew what sex was and I didn't. It made me very sexually curious, but it also made me very fearful of it. I spent my entire adolescence being curious yet avoiding sexual contact.

I was naive about sexuality, and it was a sexual experience. That is a real important aspect of sexual assault. In addition to everything else, sometimes there are sexual responses. For a child who doesn't know about these things, it is an added layer to be dealt with. The body responds in certain ways whether you like it or not. I wish I had gotten some information. The real regret is that I was never able to integrate his experience. It always stood out as an isolated event. I never really learned from it, except for things that made life harder. For a long time I thought of sex as something that happened to you. I saw myself as passive, because that had been my experience.

My sexual development has always been very painful. I never had the wonderful world of human sexuality and pleasure and fun. It opened up a very painful, confusing, and agonizing world for me that stayed terribly agonizing for an awfully long time. It has taken years of reflection, therapy, and all kinds of things to sort it out. I am really hit with the significance of this experience in my life. So much of what I thought, how I dealt with and how I saw myself really emanated from that experience. It certainly gives me great pause when I think of that.

N.

My father bothered everyone of us at some time or another. I, being the oldest, got off lightly because by the time he was into this compulsively I was fifteen. He and I had this famous thing of going dancing together a lot. It started when I was three. I literally knew the cha-cha when I was three. I don't know whether it was Christmas or Thanksgiving; I was in prep school then. I wasn't aware of what he was doing to my sisters. We were dancing in the living room, which was a common family thing on holidays. My mother was putting some of the little ones to bed. He tripped me onto the couch and landed on top of me. He was very drunk. He started pawing at my clothes and squirming around. I just started yelling, "Ma, get this drunken fool off of me." She came running out of the bedroom and between me doing what I would guess we would call a ground escape and her pulling, we pushed him onto the floor. She put him to bed and told him in no uncertain terms that he was a disgusting drunk. She was furious at him. She said, "Get off of her. What do you think you are doing? This is disgusting!" That was my only incident. I was very lucky because she was right there. I was old enough to say, "He couldn't have gotten it up if he tried. Is that what he was doing?" That kind of an attitude. It was sad. His drinking was really horrible at that point. When he was drunk he wasn't fun to dance with anymore. He would just squirm around. It wasn't very sexy what he was doing. It was just disgusting and pathetic. It embarrassed me to see him that way. What that experience probably meant most to me was that it was the end of our dancing together. He would always be drunk and disgusting. Those wonderful evenings of going out and dancing with my tall, elegant, wonderful, brilliant father were gone.

A.

There's a part of me that is feeling, oh, it's nothing. My father isn't even alive anymore. Then there is a part of me that feels, what if nothing really happened? What

a betrayal. Betraying someone when you don't even know
is a very heavy thing.

In sixth grade a couple of my friends told me that
they didn't want to come over anymore because my father
was kissing them. They told me he was doing that in a
corner of my room. It wasn't just a kiss at the door. I
don't know what he was doing. They said "kissing." I
didn't think in terms of anything else at that time. I didn't
know what they meant, but I knew it was dirty and bad.
They weren't going to come over anymore. They didn't
like it, whatever it was. I told my mother. I talked to
her through the bathroom door. I was ashamed. I felt
like it was my reputation and somehow my pride. I told
my mother that my father was kissing my friends. She
said, "Kisses are nice." I said. "My friends don't like
it. I want you to tell Daddy to stop it." She said she
would. I trusted that. One of my friends I continued to
see, but another—we just weren't friends anymore. I
thought it was me. I attributed everything to me at that
time in my life. Something was wrong with me.

I remember thinking I didn't want to be a daughter.
I felt like he was doing these horrible things. People
couldn't come over anymore. I felt like he was ruining
things for me. I felt bad for my friends. I thought it was
disgusting. I didn't think it was sex. I really didn't know
what sex was. Maybe I was naive. I just knew there was
innocuous "hello, how are you" kissing; and then there
was dirty "I'm not coming over anymore" kissing. After
a while I stopped thinking about it.

Recently my mother told me that my father had severe
sexual problems. They almost never had sex. He didn't
like anyone touching his body. He was impotent. I remembered saying to my mother, "I'm surprised I was
born." My mother said she felt inadequate and rejected.
You look at that profile of my father; it doesn't look
good. It doesn't point to very good things.

I don't know if my father did anything to me. I think
what he did to my friends was worse. I just don't know.
I think about it a lot. What was he doing, what was he
doing? There are a lot of flashes. It is all so confusing.
I don't know if everyone feels that way about their father.

I would say to an adult thinking that something happened that it is really hard, but you have those suspicions for a reason, even if you never, never really know. Trust yourself. When everyone around you is telling you the world is one way and all your perceptions and experience tell you it is different, trust yourself.

C.

I knew it was wrong, but it was exciting. I don't think it has affected me. Would I ever do that to a little boy? Of course not. It is not fair. Certainly not that young. A child is a child until eighteen, yes? There comes a time in a child's life when he or she is able to reason and that's called consent. I did consent. Though I would say to another little boy, if it confuses you, stop it.

If someone was going to do the same thing to a nine-year-old boy I'd tell him no. A child has to grow up enough to decide on his own. I feel like I grew up too fast, because I can't get back that lovely feeling. You can never return. I feel like he loved me. I don't think anything ever replaced that. I missed him psychologically. If none of that had happened, if he had given me affection without sex, I probably wouldn't think that sex, 99 percent of the time, is dirty. I can't even imagine a minister, for example, and his wife having sex and it being totally clean. I do not desire long-term relationships. Emotionally, I can't deal with it. I can't get that close.

If I had a son in the exact same position I was in and if he told me what was going on, I would tell the man, "Don't let it happen again." If he said the kid enjoyed it I'd slap him across the face.

If a little boy asked me how to start having sex and when, I would tell him to start when he was at least a teen, it should be with a girl, it should be beautiful and wonderful. There is enough time to decide whether you want to be straight or gay.

F.

It was the school bus driver who took us to Catholic school. I know he talked to me, but I don't remember what he said. I remember coming home crying and my mother asking me what was wrong. I said I felt sick. I remember the bus turning the corner and seeing my mother standing there waiting for me. I could see her while this man's hand was in my panties. I knew it was wrong. She was always very protective. I was afraid of her finding out. I knew that even whenever a kid made fun of me she would be as crazy as a lioness. But I knew this was different.

I thought I was the only one, the only kid to go through that. I thought that until after college, when I was talking to a group of friends and all of us had had some experience like that. It was great to talk about it, to find out I wasn't the only one.

I would love to beat the hell out of that bus driver, to have him understand how it feels to be powerless and unable to do anything about it. It affects my relationships with men because I think child molesters are so normal, more so than any other criminal. You don't even know who the enemy is. Like the *Invasion of the Body Snatchers*—they look like everyone else. For all I know, my boyfriend could be a child molester. You just don't know. It took me a long time to have a real personal relationship with a lover.

I would tell parents that other people will be able to control their children as much as they themselves control them. I don't mean no guidance and limits, but don't annihilate a kid's right to be a kid and to choose. The most important thing to teach children is the word *no*.

I wish that child molesting wasn't so much in the closet. I wish that every single woman on the planet would finally admit that it happened. People need to know that it happens all the time.

L.

I think for a long time I blamed myself. I should have handled it better. I could have; I should have. I wouldn't have gone through all those crazy years. Now, when I look at kids that seem about five years old, seeing how little and powerless they are, they are still babies. Then I become a little bit more forgiving toward myself. Unblocking was the probably the best thing that ever happened. The rape was the worst thing, unblocking it was the best. I think of how many people are walking around not knowing, just thinking they are crazy, like I did.

It was the first few weeks of kindergarten and my teacher punished me for talking. She told me that I was bad for talking and that I wasn't going to be able to come back to school anymore, that I had better learn to behave or I wouldn't be allowed back. I ran out of the classroom and into the schoolyard. That's where it happened. I didn't know what to do. I couldn't tell anybody. My concept was that God had punished me. God will catch you; you are never bad without being punished. I thought it happened because I was bad. I had been rude to the teacher. I had done other things at that time that I thought were bad. I guess I felt I deserved it in a way.

I don't think anyone can live a normal life by just putting it away. It affects everything you do. Everytime I start seeing a man, I'm terrified. I wonder if it will be painful, if I will be overpowered, if I'll have flashbacks. I have a lot of flashbacks having sex. It doesn't matter if I am with a man or a woman.

I remember sitting in a group. This woman was describing being raped as a child. I hadn't remembered at that point, but I wanted to say, that happened to me, too. I was freaking out inside thinking, I know exactly what you mean. Then in a self-defense class the teacher was in front of me holding a target and I kept thinking, I can't run anymore. I can't run anymore. I was being chased in the schoolyard. For a long time I kept thinking I was making it up and getting more and more flashbacks and thinking, now I have really gone crazy, imagining details of something that didn't happen.

If I could have told someone it would have made it real. I just always believed I was crazy. I still feel like a Martian. I feel like I am on this planet but I am different from everybody else. I just don't fit in. This has been my main struggle. I want to be here, like everybody else. I don't want to be different. The most important thing to tell kids is that you are not crazy and you are not responsible and that you can be OK and better and stronger. It is a lot of work, but don't give up.

E.

I try to accept my parents' limitations, but they just weren't supportive. The only thing that my mother said to me, and she should have known better, she was a

social worker, was, "Don't tell anybody, people will
think you are bad and that it is your fault." My father
took this liberal attitude: It is society's fault, this man
was oppressed. I wanted him to say, "I'm going to kill
him." I wanted someone to be angry for me, because I
wasn't angry. I went to a doctor. He said, "Do you know
how lucky you are? It's as if a bus was just about to run
you over and it just hit your little toe." I thought I wasn't
allowed to feel anything, because "nothing" happened to
me.

My parents stopped being affectionate with me after
that, especially my father. They must have changed in
themselves. I try to imagine what went on between them.
They must have talked about it. Maybe they didn't, I
don't know. I changed toward my father. I'm still working on that. He called me up around the tenth anniversary
of my rape. He said he had seen this play about rape
and realized that it would have upset me. Then he said,
"It was just about this time of year wasn't it?" It was the
first time he had brought it up. I just started crying.
Throughout my whole adolescence and up to now I have
been very angry at him. I never knew how he felt, except
that my sister told me, "You know Daddy felt horrible
that he couldn't talk to you about it." It is just starting
to heal.

I think the most important thing for adults is not to
be scared of your children. Don't back off and say, "How
horrible. I don't know what to say. I can't talk about it
because I am embarrassed." You have to give totally of
yourselves, really allow the experience, be loving and
supportive. I would say to a child, "This happened to
you, but it has nothing to do with you. It is not your
fault. Honey, you can hate this man, you can hate him
with every bit of your passion and know that you are
fine and love yourself and know that people love you."
If someone had done that for me, I think I would be
years ahead of where I am now. I had years of repression
and feeling horrible before realizing that it wasn't my
fault.

O.

I thought it was terrific. I was warm. It was the first
time my stepfather had shown me any real affection.

That lasted about five minutes, until I realized what he really wanted. When I thought about it afterward I decided I didn't like it. I also thought it was illegal. I never wondered why he did it. I didn't feel bad or guilty. It was a situation that came up and I did it after looking at the options. That was all. All according to the options. The options were those horror-show foster homes and all the publicity and what would happen at school. I told a friend of mine in the fifth grade, a very close friend. He thought I was a liar. It was clearly beyond his conception. I never mentioned it again. He told me not to tell my mother.

In my day and age nobody believed you. Compliance was the only option I had. I didn't want the marriage to break up. As far as I knew any other alternative was worse. I just got through it. I made myself more independent. I made myself incredibly self-reliant. I was an only child. I had to figure out for myself what I wanted. I really wanted to graduate from high school and split. I figured I had to get a high school diploma in order to get a job. So I did. After I left I had to rebuild my life. All I had been doing all those years was treading water. It took me about twenty years to get myself together. I'm twenty years behind where I should be.

I kept wondering why. I was just an innocent little boy. I was not doing anything to cause that. They had every power in the world over my being. What would have made it better? What would I say to a kid in that same situation now? I don't know except to tell him that I had been through it. I would offer him my apartment, but that won't work. The parents would tell him he has to come home. Then he would be in the same situation. If I could give a kid any power in the world I would give kids the power to be able to walk away.

U.

I was bleeding a little. I hurt a little. I just went back and crawled into bed. I guess it conditioned my attitude about men and sex. This was the big deal that everyone was talking about? This was sex? It was easier to make it sex than rape. It never occurred to me; I never allowed myself to think that I had been raped. I really mean it, until I was thirty. That is when I started saying, "I was

sort of raped when I was sixteen." I knew him so well;
I had admired and looked up to him for years. I thought
maybe I was flirting with him, maybe I was a sexy little
sixteen-year-old. I didn't know about rape and violence.
Rape had to do with sex for me then. I don't believe I
had ever heard the word *rape*. I don't think I knew the
concept. If I did have a concept, it was something Nazis
did to women.

My response was to choose, supposedly, choose to
continue with it. I imagine it would have continued
whether I chose it or not. I never thought of that until
this minute. But I imagine it would have happened repeatedly, possibly more forcefully. It was my first sexual
experience. I didn't quite know what he was doing, not
really. My response was, Is this what everyone makes
such a big deal about? It seemed so stupid. I was a rebel;
now I was one of the few non-virgins. You see I wasn't
saying it was rape. I said I had my first affair. I never
told anybody that I didn't enjoy a minute of it the entire
time. I couldn't understand why everyone was making
such a big deal about this sex thing. I thought this must
be something that boys were into, that it didn't really
apply to girls.

I am glad, looking back, that I was allowed not to
see it as rape until I was old enough to handle it, because
the support wouldn't have been there. It would have been
much worse for me if I had tried to deal with it as rape.
I didn't have a choice. Seeing it as sex and having it
condition my attitude wasn't a choice.

H.

Every morning I would get a seat on the subway and
look up to see a man exposing himself to me, always
the same man. I asked my parents to help me; if one or
the other would ride with me, at least for a few days,
the man would leave me alone. Each of my parents
refused. I was only fourteen. To me, this man was a
monster, larger than life and infinitely threatening. He
was part of my life for only a short time. Why does he
continue to live in me? When I sat down to write about
this, I believed that my goal was to exorcise this monster.
But who is it really? Was it the mother who cautioned

me against defending myself? The mother who said that feeding her sons breakfast was more important than protecting her daughter? My mother warned me that if I screamed the man might ejaculate on me. I didn't know what ejaculate was, but I was positive I did not want it. I had an idea that whatever it was, there was a tremendous amount of it, that I would not be able to clean myself off and still get to school. That was important. I was a "good kid," never absent, never late, a model student. Maybe the monster was my father who told me I had to learn to take care of myself. Why? Because he did not care enough about me to get up a little earlier. Eventually, someone stopped my tormentor on the train. A teenage boy pushed him off at one of the stops. He never bothered me again.

My fear was not so easy to stop. The fear has remained my constant companion. It is dying now. It has been pulled apart and the fragments are fading from memory, but the pain lives on. I laugh at it now because I understand that the pain will soon go away and never return.

S.

I was eleven and she was thirty. She was our live-in housekeeper. When she heard people approaching, she leaped out of bed real fast, so there was an aura of "this is wrong." I didn't tell anyone at that age. Her jumping out of bed like that gave me all the signal I needed that this was confidential. It wasn't unpleasant, but there was something in the secretiveness that left a bad taste in my mouth and a bad feeling about sex. I haven't really thought about it much. It has been a sort of funny little anecdote until you asked me to do this interview.

I would have liked someone to tell me I wasn't bad. I recall my early sexual experiences being attached to bad feelings. I remember having a bad feeling and not knowing where it came from. That certainly wasn't in the spoken attitude of my family. I didn't trust myself much around sex. When I was aroused, I would do things that seemed at the time perfectly all right, then as soon as the arousal was over, suddenly a lot of things seemed wrong with it. I didn't trust myself. I would be afraid to act on my feelings when I was aroused because I learned it wasn't going to be connected with how I felt later. There was a lot of confusion around that. Trusting women I was romantically or sexually involved with was always difficult. I don't know how much of that is connected to the experience. Maybe I just didn't *feel* bad; maybe there was something bad in it that I didn't understand. I guess sex is such a powerful thing. At that age it is even more powerful. There is something very unbalanced about my housekeeper's experience and mine that so easily could have left me with the feeling of not having a choice in that situation. If someone had helped me understand what was wrong with it, I could have learned something from it. I would have been a lot better off.

D.

My father was always climbing into bed with my sister. I started finding this out in my teenage years. It is hard to remember how clearly. I knew it then. I know it clearly now. Now I know why when my younger sister was twelve or thirteen she came to stay with me. When I called my father to take her home, she pleaded and cried and said, "Don't send me back. You don't know what it's like there." I think my mother knew, but I just don't think she was conscious. It is one of the wonderful things about your book, people will be much more conscious.

So much of my sister's relationship with me has been conditioned by that. I think in some ways she probably looked to me for protection, even though she never told me. I failed to protect her. I would like to tell my sister that I'll always be sorry that I didn't know and couldn't help her. There was nobody else. She was only a little girl. Maybe your book will help other people.

G.

There was this babysitter in my early childhood that I was terrified of. I don't know why. I remember that when he used to come over I would hide underneath the piano and scream and yell. My parents used to get embarrassed because I'd put up such a fight. I was making a scene. He used to try to get me to be friendly to him in front of people—I guess he was embarrassed. I was petrified of him. Just a few years ago I saw him with his wife and two daughters. I remember thinking. Oh, my God, I feel so sorry for them. They're not safe.

If I could talk to the little girl I was, I would ask her if it was all right if I stood with her behind the piano. I would want someone to come to my hiding place. I wouldn't want to come out and talk in front of everyone. I was safest behind the piano. Outside of there wasn't safe, and certain stuff couldn't be talked about. I would ask, "What's wrong?" "What happened?" "What do you want done about it?" If she said, "Nothing happened," I'd say that I know she wouldn't run under the piano if nothing happened, that she didn't have to tell me, but I didn't think someone would hide if nothing happened.

If that had happened to me when I was that little girl I would have felt like I could trust that people could be there to protect me. Now when people talk about loving me there is a part of me that doesn't believe, that doesn't know what that is. Even though someone loves you, it is still up to you whether to put yourself behind the piano.

I would say to adults that demonstrating that you love your child is more than making brownies and chocolate pudding. Those things are important, but there are many things kids are saying they need. Adults have to have really big ears. I would tell kids to keep talking until somebody listens.

B.

I didn't have any memory of being sexually assaulted. The first time I had sex I was surprised that it didn't hurt, and I thought that his penis looked small. When I was pregnant, I had a lot of strange feelings. I always thought it was the pregnancy. Then when I was in labor, they strapped me down. I felt like I was being ripped apart. Suddenly I was three years old. I was crying, saying, "I'll tell my mommy. You can't do this." And then I was screaming, "Please don't kill me, I'll be good." I remembered everything.

I asked my mother about it. She said that the doctor at the time told her, "Don't talk about it. Don't let her talk about it. She'll forget it. Don't worry." I don't blame my mother, but common sense should tell you that it will come back if you don't deal with it.

WORKING TOGETHER

This section contains an interview with a husband and wife, both of whom are incest survivors. Their testimony will promote an understanding of how childhood assaults affect adult relationships. This is a situation many couples are dealing with but for which few have received help. The man is identified as "M," the woman is identified as "W."

M & W

W: I see him as passive in a lot of things. He lets people walk all over him.

M: I've never really explored it. I don't know how it has affected me. I know how it affects how she thinks of me, and I know that as a child I felt a lot of guilt.

W: I don't trust anybody. It is a problem in our relationship. Also, because his situation was with a man, I always wonder if he will change his sexuality. I always expect him to leave me. I'm always scared. It was nice when I met him, that I could tell him.

M: It took me a little while to tell her about me. She told me first. After a while I told her because there was more than one situation. When I was growing up, there was nobody I could tell. I eventually told my father. He just told me to stop it.

W: He doesn't let me know what he feels. He is distant from me. It is such a problem. I don't know where he is. I can't stand it when people take advantage of him. Whenever I see him being self-destructive I think maybe it is because of what happened to him. I question everything. It makes me crazy. It feels like people take control of him and end up getting control of my life too. We have a lot of fights when that happens. I remember when he first told me. I thought, Oh no, what have I gotten myself into? But we were already in too deep.

M: Sometimes I feel like she overreacts to things or that we see things differently. She sees people taking advantage of me when I don't. I think she sees me as a victim. She gets mad at me, but there are some things I can't control.

W: I feel like he doesn't take care of himself. I'm scared of losing him. I really need him. I don't want to lose him. I want to scream at him, "Please take care of yourself!"

M: I feel that way about her too. I worry about her sometimes. It got worse when she was mugged. I realize that anything could happen to her. There are a lot of things I think she should do, but she thinks I am trying to control her life when I say, "You should do that." When she first told me about it I can't describe how I felt. Violated comes to mind, but I know that is not the right word. There is so much we have to deal with.

W: It comes up all the time. I feel a lot of jealousy, a lot of rage. I always want to know how it is affecting us. It's there all the time. I would tell other couples that it is going to be really rough for quite a while. When the woman is screaming she is really scared. She is just a scared little kid. She doesn't want to be hurt anymore. She's just a child howling in a vacuum.

M: I would say that sometimes the reactions have nothing to do with what's going on, but it shouldn't take away from seeing the person for who they are. Sometimes I have to tell her, "I'm not your father."

W: I want a lot more affection. I need a lot of physical affection. He's not much of a talker, either. I need a lot. I never know what is going on with him. When he's not affectionate I feel rejected. We have a lot of fights.

M: Sometimes I feel if I'm just affectionate she'll want sex. There's a lot of pressure. I guess I'm a romantic. I don't want to feel like I'm part of an assembly line. I don't want pressure.

W: I feel like I'm being starved to death. I need a lot of sex. I always feel like I better take it now when he is in the mood or I won't get it later. The other thing is whenever we really, really get close, it's so scary. I've never been that close to anybody. It is such a scary thing.

M: There was a time that she said my hands looked like her father's. It was awful. I didn't know how to deal with it.

W: I even had nightmares about it, that his hands

turned into my father's, and I cut them off. I don't want
to ever feel like I'm just a body. I have to know that I
am loved. Are there really any other couples dealing
with all this?

This section contains interviews with parents currently coping with the sexual assault of a child or their child's reaction
to their own sexual assault. This painful and difficult aspect of
parenting has too long been ignored. It was the hope of those
interviewed that their statements would help other parents in
similar situations:

K.

My thirteen-year-old came through the door screaming, "Mommy, I've been raped." My first thought was,
No, she wasn't. She can't know what that means. She
appeared uninjured except her mouth was red and swol-
len. There were bruises on her neck and her clothes were
torn. I realized it could be traumatic to go through an
exam. Every doctor I called advised me to take her to
the nearest emergency room. I stayed through the complete exam. I felt numb.

I tried to sleep with her that night. We were awake
until morning. We watched old movies, talked, cried,
and even laughed. I felt such tremendous guilt, and she
tried to reassure me. We found a counselor who helped
me understand that I could not devote my life to my
daughter's safety. She needed to go back to real life. I
was terrified. The fear did not subside for months. I
worried about everyone I loved. I felt certain that tragedy
was lurking—ready to strike another dear one.

Part of her was gone forever. The attack did change
her and my relationship with her. Her safe world had
come apart. I just wanted to baby and protect her. I am
not sure I will ever truly feel safe again. It has been
tremendously painful to see innocence die that way. The
day it happened I told her that I wished it had happened
to me instead of her. I'll probably always wish that.

J.

It has been a year and a half since the horrible night
took place. There hasn't been a day that has gone by

that I have not had a bad dream or that I don't think about what has happened to me. The hardest part was telling my twelve-year-old daughter. How do you tell her that someone took advantage of her mother's sexuality? She is just learning about her own sexuality. Asking me questions about love and sex and how they work together. How do I tell her that someone raped me? I remember the day when I finally did tell her. It hurt so much. I felt she would think less of me, that I was cheap. We all picture our parents in some form as being angels. I didn't want to ruin that image. Time and nature will change it accordingly. My daughter never mentioned it to me except for once. She wanted to know if I was scared and if I felt different. Little does she know what hell I am living in. My self-esteem is very low. I see him in almost every man that comes my way. I've become more timid and defensive toward men. I don't trust them. I've become more and more protective of my child. We argue more than we ever did before. I am afraid he is watching us/her, ready to strike when she doesn't have her mother around for protection.

M.

The hardest moment was two years later. We worked so hard to deal with the nightmares and the constant fear. I had done everything I could do. I was called to come and get her. All I could think about was the old wives' tale about mother pelicans stamping holes in their breasts with their beaks so their babies can drink their blood. I thought, That is what I have done. I had given until there was nothing more for me to do. I felt like she was never going to get well. Since it happened there has not been a single moment of any waking day, there has not been an action that I have done or considered doing that has not been in light of what would be helpful to her. My way of coping with this is to try to get her to a place where she will be as strong and as functional as she would have been had this never happened. I can't accept any of the parts of her that are still weak and damaged.

All you know is that your child has been through something no child should ever have to go through. You don't know what parts of her are broken. You have to feel your way along gingerly. Suddenly she would just fall to pieces. It was like sitting on a powder keg. I would never know when she was going to fall apart. If she could just get to school and just get home that was all I asked of her. It was all I asked of her for too long. Now it is a battle to get her to do anything. I wish there was a way to say, "Go right on being tough with your kid." But I don't think there is a mother who that would get through to. I think it is the guilt. You know you are dealing with wounds, but you don't know where they are. You can't put a bandage on them. You want to heal it, like you healed everything else. I don't know how you can tell a mother to fight that instinct.

My prayer was that God would stop him from ever doing this again. It is more than I can bear to think that he is still out there and another mother and child are going through this.

In this section, children aged five to sixteen speak about their experiences of sexual assault or coping with the assault of a loved one. The interviews were conducted from three months to four years following the incidents described. All of these children were able to tell someone who believed them; they have verbalized some of their feelings and are beginning to integrate these experiences into their lives. They, and many of their parents, received therapeutic intervention and in some cases, self-defense training. It is our hope that because of this care these children will not have to carry as much of the pain for as long as the adults looking back.

T.

I always have dreams about situations I can't control. I'm always thinking I'm going to die. I'm always alone and I can't get help. When I do get to people, they can't help me. There is nothing they can do either. I am always scared and I am always running. I know dreams are the way I get it out. There is so much I can't tell people. So much they don't understand. So much I don't know how to say. Sometimes I wake scared and I don't remember the dream. That is worse because I never know when it will hit. I'd rather dream I'm going to die than not know what is scaring me. I feel like I am always scared. I have to stay on guard. I never know when

someone might jump me. I have to be careful. It can
happen anytime, anywhere. It is always there.

Everytime I see a woman or a girl with a man I think
he has a gun or a knife on her. I think that she wants to
get away, but she can't and nobody except me knows
and I can't help her. I get so scared for her, then I think
I am really crazy. I can't talk about this stuff or people
will know I'm crazy. When I am alone I can't read
newspapers or watch TV because there is always something about rape and I can't take it. When other people
are around I can pretend it doesn't bother me. I can't
pretend when I am alone. I don't want people to feel
sorry for me, especially my parents and my friends.
When I am with them I pretend it is no big deal. It is
almost a year since it happened and I'm OK. That is
what I always say when they ask, I don't want them to
treat me differently because of this. I want them to be
the same, I want to be the same.

When it was happening I thought it would never end.
Then I thought, when it does end, I'll be dead. I didn't
want to die. I hate thinking about that part of it, not
knowing if it would end, not knowing if I would die.
Now I think that I should be able to deal with anything.
After being in a situation where I could have died, nothing should bother me. I should be strong, but I don't
really feel strong. I get mad at myself for not being strong
and for being afraid. I hate it, I should be over this.
Sometimes I wish I knew someone else who this happened to. I'm not wishing for this to happen to anyone,
but I want to have someone that I know who will know
everything that I am feeling. I want somebody really
close to me to share the pain. I want to be less alone.

Q.

We were watching *Wonder Woman*. He banged on
the door and he got in. We opened the door. He had
keys anyway. He was killing her. He was beating her.
She was bleeding. He kept beating her. There was blood
all over. I stepped over the blood and I looked at her.
She was on the floor, dead. Then the cops came. They
picked me up and took me to the neighbor's house. The
neighbor cried.

My nightmares are like when my mother got dead. I

dream of her. Somebody hit her on the head and choked her and cut her. She hollers, "Call your father, call the police," and I don't know what to do. My father doesn't come to help her. Then the police come, but she is already dead, and I don't know what to do. Sometimes I dream that she is really not dead and that she's mad at me. I never can talk to anybody about this.

If I was growed up and I found a child who was hurt I'd say, "Do you want a mother? I'll be your mother." Hurt children need mothers.

V.

When I heard what happened, I was shaky and I panicked. I was nervous, I was scared, I was troubled, until I teared.

Z.

My Daddy used to beat up Mommy. Then he left. She said I would be the little man in the house now. When that bad man came, it was night. He had a knife. He tied me to the bed when he did all those things to my Mommy. She told me not to look and to pray to God. God didn't answer. I don't want to grow up to be a man. That's why I tried to cut my tinky off. Men are mean and they do bad things. I don't want to be a man. Mommy said I'll grow up to be a good man, but I don't know any.

I.

My mother became over-protective. She still is. Sometimes I feel like she won't let it end. She is so sensitive now. Everything upsets her. She is always ana- lyzing all my feelings. She's so melodramatic about it. It feels like she doesn't want to let it pass. She talks about it every chance she can. Sometimes I say things to spite her. My father and I don't talk about it, we never did really. I don't know what he thinks. He never lets anybody know his feelings. It is OK, but I don't know how it affected us.

W.

I'd tell other kids to just tell the truth even if it is painful. If they tell, there is more of a chance of getting the guy who did it. The worst part about telling is that it's embarrassing and scary in front of all those people. Sometimes I think about it because I have bad dreams. Sometimes I just think about it. When I am alone and scared and don't know what to do, I think about it. If I could talk to him and he was tied up or something so he couldn't hurt me I'd say, "Why did you do this to me? Why did you have to? How come you had to be so mean?"

Sometimes I think it is going to happen again, but with a different person. It is a good thing I told or he would just keep doing it to other kids. Then all my friends would blame me. When I was there, I knew something was going to happen, but I didn't know what. I was scared. I knew it would be bad, but I didn't know what it would be. Mothers really can't do anything. They should try to calm their child down. Some kids think their mommies can protect them, but sooner or later they find out they just can't. I don't know what my mom thinks. She never talks about it. I know she thinks about it but she keeps her feelings inside her.

When I am scared I get goose bumps, I shake, I put my knees up so I am as small as possible. I am afraid someone is going to attack me again. Now that it has happened at least I know what I am scared of. The police officer kept asking me the same questions over and over again. I was getting bored. I really didn't want to talk about it. The first time I answered the questions and the second time I did too, but the third time I just said, "I don't know."

When he said, "Don't tell anybody," I got the creeps. Then I thought that nobody would believe me because if you're a normal kid you tell lies sometimes. Then when you tell the truth they don't believe you because one time you told a lie. Even if you don't tell lies ever, sometimes they still don't believe you. Then I thought if I told he'd find out and find me and do something worse like first beating me up and then doing the same thing again. Grown-ups really believe grown-ups, but they should believe children.

I kept hoping that some innocent person like my mother or somebody would come and find me and take me away. That's what I thought, but I didn't want the police to

come. I thought they would kill me. I was doing what
he said and it was bad so I thought the police would
either put me in jail or kill me. I was only a little kid.
I didn't know what to do. I just bundle my feelings up
and put them way down deep inside. I try to think about
other things. I don't like to think about it, but sometimes
I can't help it. Sometimes when I'm walking by myself
I think somebody is following me even when nobody is
there. I keep looking back.

I don't know why the governors and mayors always
promise to protect you and to stop crime when they can't.
They shouldn't promise if they can't keep it. They're
great actors, a lot of people believe them, but they are
horrible mayors and governors. Sometimes I just feel
like I need to talk to somebody. I don't know any of my
friends that I can talk to. People don't talk about this
stuff. Nobody can see the hurt, even when it is hurting.
I feel like he took away the good things, like my hap-
piness. Now, it's changed to mixed up feelings. Sometimes I feel like I am the only kid in the world.

X.

While it was happening I thought it was going to go
on forever. I saw myself right there like it was a dream.
I saw myself from across the room. I saw it happening.
I saw myself reaching out to the dream person of me and
it was as if I was tied up and I couldn't do anything. My
mom took it harder than I did. Before that she would
always say, "Do your homework. Wash the dishes."
After that I could do anything I wanted. Ever since, I
have been treated special. I don't like being treated special because you can't do anything normal. A couple of
friends were real nice. They sat and played with me as
usual. They didn't treat me special. I'm very grateful to
those friends. They made me forget about it. If I'm
always treated special I'm always remembering it. Before
this I always said, "Why can't I be a special kid?" But
now I don't like being special.

I have a special toy. It sounds so stupid. Sometimes
I cuddle up with it. Sometimes I sit on it because I'm
angry and I can't get my feelings out or I hit it. My head
is usually all unclear, like it's foggy. When I sit next to

someone and I'm staring at them I can make out his face on them even if it is a little girl. His face follows me everywhere.

My dad gets mad at me sometimes because I cry. I get embarrassed to cry in front of him cause he thinks I'm this tough girl. It's hard to see a tough girl cry. Once he cried cause he got so scared for me. I would say to parents, Don't let your kid find out afterwards. Tell them before. I think if I had known I never would have let him get away with it. All these people I don't even know, know what happened to me. It makes me so nervous. I want to say to my mother, "I'm so angry at you, why didn't you stop it? You knew about it." She should have been there. I thought I was living wrong. I don't know anyone else who was attacked. I feel like I'm this little person in the corner who was attacked. Everyone stares at me when I'm in the corner. My dad shouldn't be mad at me. I thought I did something wrong. My Mom shouldn't feel so sorry for me. Just treat me normally. Don't treat me as a special little girl.

4

Naming the Problem

The subject of the sexual abuse of children raises feelings and concerns for all of us. In Chapter Two we explained our most common feelings about children and how child-rearing practices affect children's vulnerability to sexual assault. Our own feelings as adults about sexuality are tied in as well. Many adults are uncomfortable with sexual issues, particularly in regard to children. We may not know how to, nor want to, explain sexual issues to children. We may find ourselves feeling sexual toward children and not know how to handle those feelings. We may see children acting sexual and feel angry or uncomfortable. Our feelings about violence will also affect our ability to think about child sexual assault. Often we want to believe that childhood is a safe place, a time for innocence and fun. It is too upsetting to realize that children are vulnerable to assault, violence, and terrifying experiences.

In this chapter we hope to replace vague fears with facts. We will explain the most common patterns of attack against children and explore the myths and realities about victims and offenders. In order to protect children it is vital to name the problem and describe all its aspects. Given this information it becomes possible to develop practical prevention strategies. We will discuss how to assess danger and spot potentially abusive situations as well as how and when to leave children alone and in the care of others.

Some people respond to the subject of the sexual abuse of children by deciding that it doesn't happen often or that it doesn't have any lasting effect on the child. Since the victim is "only a child," he or she won't remember. They believe that the child didn't really understand what was going on and therefore the assault won't have a serious impact on the child. They succeed in convincing themselves that the problem is not really a problem.

Others feel that if a child is sexually abused it will be the most traumatizing experience in the child's life. They believe that the child is ruined forever, will inevitably become emotionally disturbed, will grow up to become a prostitute, drug addict, or an alcoholic, and will never have a "normal" sex life. They may begin to feel extremely anxious about the children in their lives and respond by becoming overprotective and transmitting to children their own overwhelming fears.

The reality is often somewhere in between. Childhood sexual assault is a life-altering experience that does affect a child. However, there are positive ways to help children cope and recover from sexual assaults. We will explain this in greater detail in Chapter Eight.

Some of us believe that all child sexual assault involves overt physical force and that the child will be obviously injured, bleeding, or bruised and have torn clothing. Others believe that the abuse is a form of misplaced affection on the part of a lonely or "dirty" old man and that the child does not experience it as forceful. Many of us have an image of a child being given candy in exchange for a kiss.

Most of us believe that a child molester will be recognizable as a "bad" person. The molester will always be a man. He will be a stranger. He will probably come from another race, class, neighborhood, or ethnic group. He will appear crazed. He will be wearing a raincoat. He will have a strange look in his eyes. He will be hiding in an alleyway. He may even be foaming at the mouth. We want to believe that the offender will look as horrible as the deed. If we believe that he is recognizable, we can figure out easy prevention strategies. In addition, we can believe that if we just tell children to look out for strangers, they will be safe.

Patterns of attack against children range from a sudden, unexpected assault to an abusive relationship that is developed and carried out over a period of years. Tactics that offenders use to gain the child's submission range from overt physical force, such as striking or choking the child, to threatening the child with a weapon or using bribes, coercion, cons, or verbal threats. Recent studies indicate that approximately 85 percent of the time the child will know the attacker to some degree.

People who sexually abuse children include total strangers;

neighbors; authority figures, such as teachers; religious leaders; people involved in the child's daily life, such as school bus drivers and store owners; doctors or dentists; friends of the family; and family members. Many people believe that strangers will use physical force against a child while acquaintances or relatives will use coercion or bribery to gain submission. It is our experience that acquaintances and relatives as well as strangers will sometimes use overt physical force to the point of physically injuring the child and that strangers as well as acquaintances and relatives will sometimes use enticement, games, bribery, and threats to trap the child into an abusive relationship.

Often the line between stranger and friend is different for children than for adults. Children will take people out of the stranger category more quickly than adults. The person who spends time talking to a child and gaining their trust will no longer be perceived as the stranger they've been warned about. Therefore, warnings about strangers not only leave children totally unprepared for an assault committed by someone they know and trust but also do not help children if the "stranger" spends time "making friends."

In stranger-to-stranger assaults the attacker often will use some kind of "test" or "con" to see how easily the child can be intimidated or to gain the child's trust. Many victims report that they had a "funny feeling" that something was wrong but thought that they were just being overly suspicious. The following are some examples of stranger-to-stranger patterns of attack:

A twelve-year-old girl was on her way to visit her aunt. As she entered her aunt's apartment building a man followed her in, held a knife to her back, and told her to come with him. He walked her several blocks to another building with his arm around her and the knife at her side. He took her to the rooftop where he raped and sodomized her. The child later recounted looking at the eyes of the other adults on the street, waiting for someone to realize that she didn't belong with this man and that something was wrong.

As this example illustrates, children believe that adults will automatically recognize a bad person or a dangerous situation and will come to their rescue. This example also illustrates that adults usually assume that children belong with the people they are with.

An eight-year-old girl was walking home from school. As she entered her building lobby a man came in behind her stating that he was coming to visit his friend John. "Do you know John?" the man asked her. "No," replied the child. "Well, it's his birthday and I'd really like to surprise him. Can you let me in?" The child opened the front door and let him in. After she let him in she realized her mother had always told her not to let strangers in and suddenly felt nervous. She went to check the mail as he went upstairs. She was about to open her apartment door when he came back downstairs and said, "John is not home. Are you sure you don't know him? Maybe your mother will know where he is." "My mom is not home," the child answered. "Well, how about your grandmother?" "Nobody is home," said the girl. At that point he pulled a knife and forced her into her apartment, where he raped her.

The girl later told her mother, "You told me never to let a stranger in, but you never told me why. You never told me what would happen. You never told me how bad it would be. If I had known I never would have let him in." This child had been warned about strangers but not about the cons they might employ or the reasons they may try to gain access.

A ten-year-old boy was playing in the park when he was approached by a man he had seen around the park before. The man asked, "Aren't you Bill's little boy?" "No, my daddy's name is Joe," replied the child. "Oh, that's right. Bill works with us also and I always get them mixed up. I work with your father and today is my day off. Is your Dad still interested in racing cars?" "No, he's not interested in cars," said the boy. "Oh, right," said the man. "That's Bill again. But he told me about you and how you like animals." "Yeah, he said he was going to buy me a snake." "Right," said the man, "now I remember. He said you really like reptiles." "Yes," said the child. "I have lots of books about dinosaurs, and my dad took me to see the reptiles at the zoo." "You know," said the man, "I have a lizard collection. Would you like to come see it? I live right nearby."

The child left, assuming he was with his father's friend. The man took the child to a nearby building through a back entrance. The child could not see the address. All the while the child was talking about how excited he was about going to see the lizards. When they got to the apartment the man closed and locked the door. The child looked around and asked, "Where are the lizards?" The man stated in a quiet voice, "I don't want to have to hurt you." He raped the child. When the child returned home he told his mother, "Daddy's friend did a really bad thing." It was not until his father told him that he had no such friend that the boy realized that he had been tricked.

This example illustrates how a stranger is able to gain a child's trust and elicit information before employing overt force. It also clarifies that some attacks are carefully planned in advance.

In acquaintance and incest situations the same range of patterns may be employed by the offender. The assailant often already has the child's trust and, in many cases, the child's love. Often the child is emotionally or financially dependent on the abuser. The following examples illustrate situations where an acquaintance or family member suddenly and unexpectedly assaults a child:

A ten-year-old girl went to her local candy store for an ice cream soda. The store owner, whom she had known for years, told her that he had some newborn kittens in the basement whose mother had been killed in an accident. He told her that he was going to try to feed them but that he needed help. He asked her if she would come downstairs and hold the kittens while he fed them. He told his assistant to mind the store while they went and fed the kittens. Once down in the basement he pointed to the corner where the kittens were. She went over to them and started playing with them. While her back was turned he locked the door and piled boxes in front of it.

When she turned to ask him how they were going to feed
the kittens, she could no longer see the door and realized
that she had been locked in. He raped her orally and
anally. He told her never to tell anyone what happened
or she would be sorry. When she went home she asked
her mother for mouthwash. She had never used mouthwash before, and her mother suspected that something
was wrong. Her mother said, "I know something is wrong.
Tell me what it is." The girl started crying and said that
she was scared. Her mother held her and let her cry.
Then the child told her what had happened. The child
later stated, "I always thought that people who took care
of animals were nice people."

As this illustrates, stereotypes of good and bad behavior
often leave children vulnerable.

Six children were playing in a yard—five boys and
an eight-year-old girl. The girl was approached by a local
teenager whom she had seen around the neighborhood.
He told her, "You are coming with me." She said, "I
don't want to." He said, "You have to." He pulled her
by the hair and dragged her out of the yard. Two of the
children ran to their mother, who said, "He's probably
teasing her. He would never really hurt her." Meanwhile,
the child's younger brother came to look for her and saw
that she wasn't there. The other children told him what
happened. He ran home and told his mother. She ran to
the teenager's house. He initially denied her daughter
was there and then let her out. When the mother asked
her daughter what had happened, she didn't respond.
The mother said, "I know something happened. You can
tell me." The girl described being raped.

This example illustrates how powerless children feel, since
six children felt unable to stop one adolescent. In addition,
having an adult be unresponsive to a direct call for help ex-
acerbated this feeling.

A seven-year-old boy was being taken care of by his
uncle. He was told he would be allowed to stay up later
than his mother allowed if he agreed to play a secret

game with his uncle. The game began with wrestling, proceeded to nude wrestling, and ended with mutual masturbation. The uncle told him that his mother would be angry at both of them if she found out and that he had better not tell. The boy felt guilty for breaking his mother's rule. Several weeks later when his uncle was going to come and babysit again, the boy started crying and said, "I don't want him to come. He is going to make me play that game again." The mother asked, "What game?" The boy answered, "You will be angry if I tell you." She promised she wouldn't be angry, and he told her.

In this, as well as the other examples, the mother's sensitivity enabled the child to disclose the incident. In addition, in this case, further abuse was prevented as the mother no longer allowed the uncle to babysit.

In the following example, the babysitter was in jeopardy:

A sixteen-year-old girl was babysitting at a hotel. The father of the children came to the room between nightclub acts to check on the children. He asked her how they had behaved. She answered fine and added that they were asleep. He started telling her how beautiful she was. She began to feel uncomfortable and asked him to leave and go back to watch the rest of the show with his wife. He came toward her and backed her into a corner. He pushed her against the wall and began to molest her. She screamed, but the children slept through the screams, and no one else was around to hear her. She calmed herself down and told him that she was going to tell everyone what he was doing and that he would be in trouble. He backed off and apologized, told her he didn't know what had come over him, and promised never to do it again, adding that she didn't have to tell anybody. She never did tell anyone, except a friend. She felt unable to tell her parents because they were both sick and she was babysitting to earn money, as they could not afford to give her any. She was afraid that if she told them they wouldn't let her babysit anymore, thereby cutting off her only source of income.

As the above examples illustrate acquaintances and relatives use a range and combination of tactics from cons to physical force to gain a child's submission during the assault and a child's silence afterwards.

In addition to sudden and unexpected assaults, there are patterns of attack that involve the development of a sexually abusive relationship over a period of time. Sometimes the relationship begins innocently and slowly becomes abusive. Usually the offender has the child's trust and faith to begin with. The following examples illustrate how these relationships develop:

A six-year-old girl was asked by the neighborhood softball coach to join his team. He gave her special lessons and made her his official assistant, a position the other children vied for. Over a period of several weeks he told her how special she was, how much better than the other children she was, and how glad he was to have her as his assistant. One day he told her he wanted to show her something special. He showed her pornographic magazines and materials and then exposed himself to her. He asked if her mother allowed her to see things like that and if she thought her mother would be mad. He told her that he was sure she would be in a lot of trouble if her mother found out and that she had better never tell. He involved her in a sexually abusive relationship that lasted four years. Whenever she tried to stop him he told her that she was forcing him to tell her mother about the kind of girl she really was. Each time she backed down and agreed to do whatever he wanted. She did not tell until she discovered that several other children had a similar relationship with him that they were trying to get out of. After she disclosed, twenty-two other children came forward, including her younger sister. The children ranged in age from four to eleven.

In this case the offender established trust and friendship through flattery and special attention. He later encouraged the children to break a rule and then threatened to expose their "bad" behavior. They were more frightened of parental disapproval than of the abuse, despite the fact that most of the parents were not harsh in their discipline. This is an example of how authoritarian adults can control a child's reality.

A ten-year-old boy was called into his father's room for a "man-to-man" talk. His father told him that he was now old enough to be prepared to be a man. His father then told him to masturbate in front of him. The boy was uncomfortable and frightened, but because of his father's violent temper he was also afraid to refuse. This relationship escalated and continued for seven years, until the boy left home. He did not disclose it until he was in therapy after his third suicide attempt at age twenty-four.

The above are examples of the range of patterns of assault against children. In addition to myths about patterns of attack, there are also myths about victims and offenders.

Some of us believe that only very attractive or seductive children will be assaulted. Others believe that sexual assault results from the carelessness of parents or that it only happens to "bad" children who are unsupervised or live in "bad" neighborhoods. Many people can accept that adolescents may be sexually assaulted but find it impossible to believe that younger children can also be victimized. As we have stated earlier in this book, studies are showing that one-fourth of all children in the United States will experience some form of sexual abuse before they are eighteen. Boys and girls appear to be at equal risk. Victims have been as young as two weeks. Children who are short or tall, healthy or sick, athletic or physically disabled, very intelligent or mentally retarded, well cared for or neglected and unsupervised can all be sexually assaulted. There is no stereotypical victim. There is no way to predict that one child will be vulnerable while another will not. There is no victim personality that invites assault, no seductive child who provokes abuse. The responsibility for the assault lies entirely with the offender. As the case examples have illustrated, just as there is no stereotypical victim, there is also no stereotypical offender. Offenders come from all different classes, backgrounds, races, religions, and ethnic groups. A child molester can be the president of a corporation or a vagrant; a trusted leader in the community known to everyone or someone lonely and isolated. Though we often believe that the child molester, having no other access to sex, turns to children out of sexual frustration, this belief is not borne out by the research currently being done with offenders. Such research shows that a large percentage of child molesters are married or in stable, long-term relationships. Whether they assault boys or girls or both, most proclaim themselves to be heterosexual. Offenders seem to commit the assaults when they are frustrated with their lives in general and feel unable to manage their anger and aggression. Assaults seem to be motivated out of a need or compulsion to manipulate, control, have power over, hurt, injure, or destroy a child.

Recent evidence is revealing that a large percentage of child molesters were themselves sexually assaulted in childhood and never received help. It appears that sexual abuse may be a cycle, repeated from generation to generation, much as physical abuse is. This does not mean that everyone who is sexually assaulted in childhood becomes a child molester as an adult. It does mean, however, that some people who are sexually abused and do not receive help will turn to committing assaults themselves as their way of coping with the trauma.

Though most reported incidents of child molestation involve male offenders, women have also been known to sexually abuse children. As more research and public education is conducted, we expect to get a more accurate picture of the number of female perpetrators.

Many children who are victimized will want to know why it happened. One of the most common questions children ask in public-education programs is, "Why do people do things like that to children?" The following testimonies will give insight to some of the issues involved in answering this question:

My father sexually abused me for years. I could never understand why because he really seemed to love my mother and have a good relationship with her. I used to obsess on trying to understand why he did it and what it was like for him. I knew that for me it was horrible, but I had to know what it was like for him. One day when I was fifteen I was babysitting for two children who were two- and four-years-old. I molested both of them. I molested the little girl first and when it felt horrible I thought it was because she was a girl and I was a girl; so I molested the little boy. That also felt horrible. I know it was horrible for me. I don't know if it was horrible for my father. I never did it again, but I wonder whatever happened to those children and how it has affected them and if they have grown up to hate themselves the way I hate myself.

While some offenders molest children only once or twice, or occasionally when they are under severe stress, most in treatment do it compulsively.

I started with my daughter when she was five. It was so easy. She let me do anything I wanted. After the third time she didn't even cry or ask me to stop. The next time one of her friends came over I tried it with her. When I was able to do that too, it became like a game, to see how many children I could do it with, how many children I could get. Some of the kids must have told, because they stopped coming around. But then I just started taking my daughter to the playground and inviting kids to join us for ice cream or candy. I wasn't caught for four years. I can't even tell you how many children I molested. It had to be at least two hundred, but I'm not really sure. After I was caught, everybody asked me why. I didn't know why; I really didn't. I'm not sure now, either. It just became so exciting to get so many kids and have nobody know.

While some offenders will say that assaulting children is exciting or a compulsion they don't understand, others are very clear on their desire to hurt or destroy.

I always hated kids, especially the happy ones. I always felt like they had something I never had, and I couldn't stand that. I used to snatch really happy, smiling children. I never said anything to them. I just took them into my car or to an isolated area and raped them. Never once did I say a word. When they were crying or screaming I knew that was it, I had won. They were never going to be happy again. They were going to be like me, no happy childhood to look back to.

It is sad that this man's only way of resolving his own tortured childhood was to resort to such destructive behavior.

All of us have unresolved feelings about painful incidents in our childhoods. As we explained in Chapter Two, all of us have conflicting feelings about children. We all get angry, have moments of frustration, have fantasies about hurting people, or thoughts about getting back at people who have hurt us. If we are going to protect children, it is important to acknowledge these feelings, learn to control and manage them in ourselves, and spot them in others.

Children cannot be responsible for setting such limits when it is adults who control the world. For this reason the offender is always responsible for the abuse no matter what the child was doing. Therefore it is important that when adults set boundaries that they consider the child's welfare before their own.

My daughter was two years old when she discovered masturbation. One day I walked into her room while she was lying on her bed masturbating. I continued what I was doing, trying to act nonchalant, when she said, "Oh, Mommy, this feels so good." I said, "That's nice." She added, "I really like it when I tickle myself there, why don't you do it, Mommy, why don't you tickle me there?" I told her it was not appropriate for mothers to do that with their children, but that it was fine for her to do it. I realized later that had I done it, had I masturbated her, I would have then had to force her to keep it secret. Eventually I would have had to threaten her to maintain the secret, and maybe she would forget it entirely and twenty years from now if she were on a psychiatrist's couch talking about the incident she would be told that she seduced her mother.

The boundaries for adult-child relationships are set by adults, not children. In the above example, the mother set the boundaries without alarming the child or creating anxiety or fear. In addition to setting limits in our relationships with children, we are often faced with having to set limits in their relationships with other adults. Parents will often feel that something may be wrong but not know how to explore their suspicions with the child. A parent may suspect that a child's relationship with another adult is becoming sexually abusive or has the potential for becoming so. Signs that this may be happening include a child talking about a secret club run by an adult or special or secret games played with a babysitter or an acquaintance; displaying presents for being special or gifts they are not allowed to tell you about; and being upset about receiving a gift or about being special or having a secret. These may all be signs that an adult is beginning a relationship with a child that will become sexually abusive.

My son was seven years old when he came home with a new blue truck. I asked him where he got it and he said he was in the "blueboys" club. I didn't think anything of it until he added, "And I can't tell you about it." I then said, "Why does it have to be a secret?" He said, "Because you can't be a blueboy if you tell the secret." I asked him if he had fun being a blueboy, and he said it was great, that he got the new truck, and that he was going to be getting a lot of other things. I asked him if there were a lot of blueboys. He said there were four altogether and one blueman. When I asked who the blueman was he identified a neighbor. Then I asked him when the club started, and he beamed as he said, "This is my first day. My friend invited me to join." I asked him why, if the club was so good, they had to keep it secret. He said that was what made it a special club. I told him that special clubs worried me because sometimes they started out being fun but they didn't always end up that way. He seemed interested in this and asked me what I meant. I said that when adults ask children to keep secrets that a lot of times it's not fair because it is very hard to keep a secret, especially from your mommy and daddy. He nodded in agreement and told me his friend had told him that he wished he didn't have to keep it secret. I asked him what made him think that keeping a secret was good. He said he didn't know if it was good but that it meant he got a new truck. I asked him what he would do if it meant he would have to do something bad or uncomfortable. He said he didn't know. I then asked him if he had asked his friend why he didn't want to keep the secret anymore. He said he would ask him. We found out later that day that his friend had been sexually assaulted, and we were able to crack a kiddie porn ring.

Escalating degrees of fears and phobias in a child may indicate that an incident has occurred or that the child is sensing

imminent danger. In one case a child began developing increasing amounts of fear over a one-year period. It began with
a fear of going to school, a fear of there being a fire at school,
and a fear of something happening on the way home from
school. Her fears then progressed to a fear of the dark, a fear
of going to sleep, and various other fears. Upon investigation,
it was learned that these fears coincided with the development
of a situation at home that seemed like the beginning of a
sexually abusive relationship with her father. During that year
he had been gradually loosening the boundaries of privacy that
had previously been set. He started walking in on her when
she was in the bathroom, coming into her room naked, and
leaving his door open while he was having sexual relations
with his girlfriend. The child had a sense that something was
about to happen, a sense of approaching danger that manifested
itself in ever-increasing fears and phobias.

In thinking further about our children's safety, we realize
that one of the questions we have is, When can we leave our
children alone or in the care of others? We need to learn to
assess the potential for danger in varying situations as accu-
rately as we can. One situation that almost all parents and
guardians face is taking a child to the doctor. Few of us recognize this as even being remotely dangerous. However, the
following testimonies illustrate the potential for abuse:

> When I was six years old my pediatrician told my
> mother that he had to give me an anal examination be-
> cause he was very concerned about the increase in colon
> cancer. He explained that this examination is often un-
> comfortable and upsetting to children and told her that
> it would be best if she left the room. He told me to be
> a good girl and not to cry. He proceeded to put his finger
> in my anus and told me he was checking me out to make
> sure everything was OK. Then he started masturbating
> me. I started to cry and asked him to stop. He said he
> had to do it, that it was for my own good. This went on
> every year until I was fourteen, when I finally rebelled
> and told my mother I would never go back to that doctor
> again. I can't believe my mother didn't realize that he
> was abusing me. Before every checkup I used to cry and
> plead. I would promise to do anything not to have to go.
> Looking back, I guess she was in awe of doctors and
> couldn't fathom that he would be abusing me.

It is best for a parent to be in the examining room with small children. As the child gets older, he or she may feel that a parent being there is an infringement of their privacy. In that case, it is important to trust your instincts and to be alert to the child's behavior after a visit to the doctor. This includes visits to eye doctors, dentists, etc., as well as to pediatricians. It is also all right to ask your child how it went, what they thought of it, was it confusing, is there anything they want explained, is there anything they want you to talk to the doctor about.

For adolescents the problem is different. Many seek medical care on their own or would be insulted if their parents accompanied them.

When I was sixteen I was sent to an orthopedic clinic for a knee problem. I was X-rayed and taken into an examining room. The resident said he had to do an examination. I was told to take off all my clothes and get up on the table. The nurse came in and gave me a hospital gown. The doctor told her to leave the room, and then he shut the door. He told me he had to give me a complete examination. After listening to my heart and looking down my throat, he told me to take off the gown and began a breast exam. It was very, very painful. He was squeezing my breasts and squeezing my nipples, but I was too afraid to cry out in pain. I kept thinking, What does this have to do with my knee? Why is he doing this? I also kept thinking that breast exams are not this painful. I couldn't tell anybody because my parents didn't know I had already been to a gynecologist and had had a breast exam. When he wanted to do a pelvic I absolutely panicked and told him I had just had one a month before and that I didn't need one. He said fine and told me to get dressed while he looked at my X-rays. When he left I started to cry. The nurse came in and asked me if I was all right. I said, "I will be," and never told anybody. I never went back; I never got treatment for my knee. I told my parents that they said that if I exercised I would be fine. For ten years I referred to it as a "painful breast exam" until a friend said, "He assaulted you—that was a sexual assault."

One mother concerned about this issue told her fourteen-year-old daughter the following: "One of the things that happens as you grow up is that you want to do more and more things without me. Sometimes even though you are older things that scared you when you were little will still scare you. For example, I am still scared of going to the dentist even though I am forty, so I always have my best friend come with me. It is a good idea if you are going to the doctor, or any other appointment that you are worried about, to have someone go with you. If you don't want me to come, I hope that you will bring a friend."

Another common situation is shopping with young children. Many adults will leave a child to play in one area of a store while shopping in another. In one case a mother left her child in the toy department while she went to a nearby clothing department. She returned shortly to find her six-year-old son gone. She asked people if they had seen him, and they replied that his father had picked him up. The child had been screaming as the man who identified himself as his father carried him away. Witnesses assumed that the child was just having a tantrum. The child was found dead several days later. It is never safe to leave a small child without a trusted guardian, even in a semipublic or public area.

Choosing a babysitter is a common problem. Whether we leave our children with a relative or a local teenager, we need to take certain safety precautions. One is to tell the child clearly what the rules are and to repeat the rules to the sitter in front of the child. For example, "Jane has already had her bath. She always puts her pajamas on by herself and doesn't need help. She is to go to bed by eight and not to stay up later than that for any reason." This minimizes the risk of abuse resulting from the sitter trying to give Jane another bath, insisting on helping her undress, or offering to let her stay up late in exchange for playing a secret game. In addition, we need to be alert to children's responses to babysitters. If a child seems afraid or nervous when a particular sitter is coming, we should not assume that the child is just upset that we are going out. We need to try to find out what is going on, and change sitters, even if we cannot ascertain what is happening.

My three-year-old daughter became hysterical every time the girl I had hired as a sitter was to come over. I thought maybe the sitter didn't pay enough attention to her and never thought much of it. I mentioned this to my pediatrician, who said, "Fire that sitter immediately and get another one." Up until the time he said that it never occurred to me that the girl might be mistreating my daughter. I did fire that sitter and found one my daughter is comfortable with.

After learning about the patterns of attack and understanding how to assess danger, the next step is to begin discussing these issues with children and developing self-protection strategies with them.

5

Talking About the Problem

Most adults are hesitant to talk to children about personal safety because the subject is so upsetting and raises so many concerns. Few of us have been given the information needed to adequately discuss the problem with children. When we do seek out the information we often find it to be limited and impractical due to the myths and misconceptions examined in the previous chapter. To compensate for our fears and lack of information we create magical "safety bubbles" such as: "Our neighborhood is safe." "My child is careful." "Those things don't happen to people you know." "If I don't think about it, it won't happen." "I never leave my child alone." "My child doesn't talk to strangers."

The problem with these safety bubbles is that they create a false sense of security. We periodically hear of a child in the neighborhood being victimized or read in the papers of a situation that we know our child could have been in. Each time this happens we are frightened and confused. We try to deny that our magical safety bubble has burst and try to push these thoughts out of our minds. These feelings lead us to develop rationales for not talking to children about their personal safety. Although it is clear from the way in which we teach fire and traffic safety that it is best for children to be alert to danger, in the area of crime avoidance our systems of rationales and denial inhibit us from comfortably addressing these issues and taking practical prevention measures.

Some of the common rationales are illustrated by the following examples:

"It makes me feel so uncomfortable."

Jane, an elementary-school teacher, herself molested at age eight by her uncle, found it impossible to talk to her students about personal safety. She was afraid talking to the children would remind her of her own experience and unresolved feelings.

"Won't it make them paranoid?"

Steve, a father of two, was recently mugged. Since then he has become greatly concerned about crime but finds the more he reads and hears about it, the more upset he becomes. He wants to protect his children from these feelings of anxiety and fear.

"Aren't they too young to learn about sex?"

Mary, a mother of three, was raised in a family where sex was a taboo subject. For her, talking about preventing sexual abuse would mean introducing the subject of sex to her children. She finds this idea too embarrassing and disconcerting.

"Won't they start misinterpreting everything?"

Rebecca, a pediatrician, was assaulted when she was a teenager. She spent many years trying to recover from the effects of the assault, the most devastating of which was her discomfort at being touched. She's concerned that children will have a similar reaction if the subject of sexual assault is even mentioned.

"They'll lose their innocence."

David, a police officer, believes that children's lives should be as carefree as possible. He feels that talking to them about personal safety is an unnecessary introduction to the adult troubles they will have to face soon enough, anyway.

"They can't protect themselves anyway, so what's the use?"

Nina, a mother of two, was assaulted six months before she asked this question. She had been cautious and aware of street safety, only to be attacked in her own home by a neighbor. Unable to prevent her own assault, she could not imagine how her children could be anything but helpless.

"Won't they start courting danger?"

Linda, a grandmother of three, was a brazen and rebellious

adolescent. She is fearful that if her grandchildren are given self-protection information they will take unnecessary risks and have a false sense of safety.

"It's just too much! How can I begin?"

Edward, a father of two, feels completely overwhelmed by the whole subject. He puts off even broaching the topic with his children, fearing that he will take on more than he knows how to handle.

In order to begin communicating with children, we need to learn to speak their language. It is important to realize the vocabulary differences between children and adults. These differences vary depending on the child's age and upbringing. However, listening to what the child is saying and how it is being said is crucial. If the child's anxiety seems inappropriate to the content of his or her statement, it is necessary to explore further. Many of the children we have worked with did not get help initially because they used words such as "bother," "tease," and "funny game" when they meant fondle, molest, and coerce. The following case history tragically illustrates this point:

> Jane was seven years old when she told her mother, "Uncle Joe always teases me, especially when he is babysitting for me." Her mother replied, "Oh, that's part of growing up. My uncle used to tease me, too." Jane's eyes widened and welled with tears as she asked, "But, Mommy, how could you stand it?" "Well, I just learned to live with it, I guess," her mother answered. Jane then burst into tears and her mother comforted her. Six months later Jane was diagnosed as having gonorrhea of the throat.

It is unfortunate that Jane's mother didn't know how to explore what her daughter meant by the word "teasing" or why she burst into tears. The following is an example of how she could have handled the situation:

Jane: Uncle Joe always teases me, especially when he is babysitting for me.
Mother: Does it bother you?
Jane: Yes, I hate it.
Mother: Does he tickle you or say things that upset you?

Jane: Well, sometimes he wants to play funny games and I don't want to.

Mother: What kinds of games?

This type of questioning can be pursued until the child's statement is clarified.

Communicating effectively with children also includes knowing how to interpret their behavior. Many children are unable to express themselves verbally either because they are too young or they don't have the words to describe what is bothering them or are so upset they cannot verbalize their feelings. It is important to be alert to sudden changes in children's behavior and to behavior that seems inappropriate in a given situation. The following is an example of how one mother was able to discover that her two-year-old daughter was receiving corporal punishment from her grandfather:

An hour and a half after Lynn returned from visiting her grandfather, she began hitting her favorite doll. This was highly unusual behavior for her, prompting her mother to say, "Lynn must be very upset or angry if she is hitting Tina." Lynn stopped and looked up at her mother, who then asked her, "Is that true Lynn, are you upset or angry? It's OK to let Mommy know." Lynn came over to her mother and said, "Bapa." (Her attempt at Grandpa.) Her mother asked, "Are you upset with Grandpa?" Lynn repeated "Bapa" and then hit herself on the arm. At that point her mother asked, "Did Grandpa hit you?" Lynn began to cry. Her mother soon confirmed that Lynn had been hit several times by her grandfather during her visit. Lynn's mother told her, "Grandpa had no right to hit you. Mommy is angry with him and will tell him not to ever do it again." Thus, even nonverbal children can communicate what is happening to them and are able to get help, if adults are sensitive to the barometer of their behavior.

Communicating effectively with children requires less effort if a mutual vocabulary is established. It is particularly important to name body parts. The actual words are not as important as a mutual understanding of what they mean. If a child knows and understands the words, it will be easier to communicate a physical violation. One father explained this to his four-year-old daughter in the following way: "The parts of your body covered by your bathing suit are private. Someone may try to touch your private parts or ask you to touch theirs. That is not fair and they shouldn't do that. If that happens, I want you to tell Mommy or me."

Often children are more concerned with crime than the adults around them realize. Television programs and magazine or newspaper articles can be used as starting places to find out how much a child knows and to begin to provide accurate information. For example, when ten-year-old Sara brought an article about rape to her current events class, her teacher asked the children what they thought the word "rape" meant. After receiving definitions such as "Rape is when you are kidnapped and murdered" and, "Rape is when a man makes a woman pregnant," she explained that there are various types of assault, and when someone forcibly touches or assaults your private parts it is called a sexual assault or rape.

A mother whose eight-year-old son asked, "Why would someone do that?" answered in the following way: "It's a way of hurting someone. There may be a person who is hurting inside and wants to hurt someone else. Rape is a way to hurt someone else, and no one will know unless that person tells. It's not like if you punch somebody; then they will have a bruise. If you cut somebody, they will bleed. If you push someone down, they might get hurt. But if you touch somebody when they don't want to be touched or kiss them when they don't want to be kissed, you can be hurting them—and no one will know unless they tell."

In addition to examining how we communicate with children, the content of what we are communicating must be explained. A common concept many of us have been taught is that if we are good we will be rewarded and if we are bad we will be punished. We have a need to believe that there is justice in the world and a need to impart this belief to children, perhaps in the hope that it will become true. This belief also helps us to control children through threats of punishment and the power to tell children if they are good or bad. But there is no justice when it comes to assaults on children. Assaults on children are committed by good and trusted people, happen in good and safe places, and happen to good children. If children who have been told that if they are good they will be rewarded and if bad, punished, are assaulted, they will be forced to conclude that they must be bad or this bad thing wouldn't have happened to them.

A child who has been raised to be good, in the traditional sense, is often an easy target for the child molester. Dr. Gene Abel, a nationally known psychiatrist who treats child molesters, quoted one of his patients as saying that he picked children as victims because they never said no to adult demands. It is important to teach children that good and bad are not rigid concepts: "People are never completely bad nor completely good. Sometimes good people will try to hurt you." Children will know this from their experiences with peers. Friends who are nice to them some of the time will bully them at other times.

Children should be told that "just because someone is your friend or a friend of the family doesn't mean they have the right to hurt you. Good people sometimes get hurt by others or are in a bad mood or get angry and then try to take it out on a child. They don't have the right to do this, and you have the right to stop them." This training will help a child prevent abuse, particularly when the abuser is loved and trusted by the child. It will also help the child put the assault into a manageable context. It may be intolerable to the child to think of the abuser as a "bad" person; additionally, such a concept could destroy the child's faith in his or her own judgment and instincts.

Children can also be told, "If someone you love hurts you it doesn't mean you made a mistake in trusting them. It means they did something wrong, something they shouldn't have done. It is their responsibility to control their hurt or angry feelings, and it's not your fault if they don't." Children see injustice all around them. They know that being smaller and weaker means being bullied and picked on. They know that being a child involves limited power and control.

It is important to admit to ourselves and our children that the world is not always a fair place. This can be explained in the following way: "Sometimes things happen for no reason. Remember when Uncle Sam was in a car accident? He hadn't done anything to deserve being hurt; it was an accident. Crime works the same way. Sometimes people are attacked. They don't deserve to be, and there isn't any reason why it happens to them." This type of explanation is the means by which children can learn to cope with reality and thus learn how to protect themselves from danger.

A child who is especially fearful of punishment or of being labeled "bad" is a child who can become an easy target for abuse, as the following case history illustrates.

> A twelve-year-old girl was cáught sneaking into a local movie theater without paying. The manager took her into his office and said, "I should call your parents, but you are too old for that. Let's make a deal." Whereupon he molested her and added, "Next time you want to come in for free, come and see me first." This child didn't disclose the incident for two years, fearing her parents would be angry that she had done something wrong and feeling as if she had deserved what happened as punishment.

It is also important to realize that all children at times break our rules or do something wrong. It is necessary to let them know that if they do it doesn't mean they are "bad" people, that we won't love them anymore, or that other people have the right to punish them: "You know how I always tell you that you are not allowed to go into the park by yourself? I made that rule because I am afraid of what can happen if you do. Well, maybe one day you will break that rule. If you do, and something happens, I will be angry that you broke the rule, but I won't blame you for what happens. I will be upset and concerned that you are hurt, and I hope that you will feel that you can come to me for help."

After we address and redefine some of the traditional concepts by which we raise children, the next step is to create new ways of raising children that minimize their risk of becoming victims. In our experience with children we have found that patterns of attack correspond directly to a child's conditioning. Often the more we try to make our child "good," the more vulnerable he or she becomes. Children need to be given rights over their bodies and feelings in order to be able to prevent abuse. The following list is a guide. It is applicable to children of all ages and is interpreted in different ways to children of different ages. The following rights are crucial to a child's safety. Without them a child will not be able to adequately follow safety regulations or apply safety principles to different types of situations.

A CHILD'S BILL OF PERSONAL SAFETY RIGHTS

1. The right to trust one's instincts and funny feelings.
2. The right to privacy.
3. The right to say no to unwanted touch or affection.
4. The right to question adult authority and say no to adult demands and requests.
5. The right to lie and not answer questions.
6. The right to refuse gifts.
7. The right to be rude or unhelpful.
8. The right to run, scream, and make a scene.
9. The right to bite, hit, or kick.
10. The right to ask for help.

When introducing these rights to children, it is important to use language that is comfortable for us and understandable to the child and to be as concise and concrete as possible. The following are explanations and examples of how to introduce these rights.

The Right to Trust One's Instincts and Funny Feelings

Most of us have bodily warning signals that tell us when we are in danger. Children usually have a physical response to stress: heart pounding, stomachaches, pounding in the ears, breathing difficulties, shaking hands or knees. Any of these can be the body's clue that something is wrong. The child may not be able to define his or her fears but may feel something bad is about to happen. It is important to tell children to trust their sense of reality and their instincts—no matter how silly they feel and no matter what anyone else tells them: "Did you ever have a funny feeling but didn't know what was the matter? Those feelings are called instincts, and they are usually the way your body tells you that something is wrong."

The Right to Privacy

It is important to give children the sense that they own their bodies and to help them develop a sense of privacy and bodily integrity. Every household has different rules about this. A good guide is to give children the same set of privileges the adults have, except in cases where the child's physical safety would be in jeopardy. For example, an infant cannot bathe him/herself, but a four-year-old should be allowed to close the bathroom door when using the toilet. In many intrafamily sexual-abuse situations the abuse begins with the abuser insisting that he or she bathe the child or insisting that the child undress in front of him/her or keep the bathroom door open, when it is not the child's choice nor necessary for the child's safety. We should not assume that children do not have a sense of privacy. Many do; however, their wishes are often not respected and are sometimes laughed off as "cute."

The Right to Say No to Unwanted Touch or Affection

This is an extension of a child's right to privacy. In our society it is often assumed that adults, particularly family members and authority figures, have the right to touch children whenever they want to, with or without the child's consent. Children are picked up, tickled, hugged, kissed, cuddled, and pinched at the whim of the adults around them. By the time the average child reaches adolescence, s/he has learned that they have no control over when they are touched. If children do not have the right to say no to unwanted touch or affection, with adult backing, they will be unable to prevent sexually abusive situations. There are several ways to begin communicating this to children at a young age. The following are two examples:

Grandma to child: Come and kiss me goodbye.
Child: I don't want to.
Grandma: What! Don't you love me? Be good and come give me a kiss.
Mother to child: If you don't want to kiss Grandma goodbye you don't have to. Would you like to shake her hand or throw her a kiss or just say goodbye from where you are?

This mother clarified for her child that one can love someone without submitting to unwanted physical affection.

Magic Circle Game This is a game that adults can play with an individual child or a group of children. A child stands in the middle of the room. Another player, child or adult, approaches the child from the front. At any point, the child can say STOP. The approaching player must freeze and not come any closer to the child. This gives the players the experience of having their limits respected as well as respecting others' limits. This game can also be played with the child in the middle being approached from behind. In this case, the child says STOP as soon as s/he feels the presence of the approaching player. This sharpens a child's instincts about being followed or being approached from behind.

Children may find it easier to tell a child to stop than to say it to an adult. This difficulty can be discussed. The game is explained to children in the following manner: "Each of us has a magic circle around us that no one can see. No one should be allowed to cross our magic circle unless we want them to. Our magic circle is probably very wide for people we don't know who bother or scare us and very small for people we love. This is a game to help you keep your magic circle."

Many adults are concerned that this type of training will make a child reject any kind of affection. It is our experience that affection and physical contact are basic human needs. Children will seek out affection when they want it and respond positively when it is provided for them. We should not limit the spontaneity of our affection, but we must become sensitive to the child and not impose our needs when children clearly demonstrate that they do not want to be touched. One mother, intuitive to her daughter's needs, related the following: "She looked so hurt for days after she was assaulted. One day when we were talking about it I just wanted to hold her, but I wasn't sure if that was what she needed. So I just said, 'I really feel like I want to hug you. Would you like that now?' She said, 'I really don't want to be held or hugged right now,' and added, 'I'm sorry.' I told her not to be sorry, that it was important for her to decide when she wanted to be held or touched. Then I offered to hold her hand whenever she needed it. She immediately took my hand, and I held it, pretending to myself that it was the hug I so desperately needed to give her."

The Right to Question Adult Authority and Say No to Adult Demands and Requests

We may want to believe that adults will never misuse their authority over children, but the patterns of attack demonstrate that this misuse is quite common. While teaching children to respect authority, we must also teach them to protect themselves from those who misuse it. Children's rights to trust their instincts, maintain their privacy, and say no to unwanted touch or affection are rights that hold with authority figures such as teachers, medical personnel, store owners, clergy, and anyone else who has authority over children. Just as we explain to children that no one is completely good or bad, we need to explain that authority figures and role models are not perfect. Authority figures will sometimes use their right to reward or punish as a way of manipulating a child into submission. Teaching a child to say no challenges our desire to control children but ultimately helps insure their safety in the world. Children need to be taught that they have the right to say no to an adult demand or request if their instincts tell them the demand or request is wrong. The following is an assertiveness exercise that is useful for teaching children this skill.

Saying No Exercise In this game an adult asks a child or group of children a series of questions. The adult progresses from being reasonable and friendly to using guilt-inducement and threats in order to gain compliance. The child maintains steady eye contact and responds to each request or demand with an unqualified no. The child is not allowed to make excuses or offer apologies.

Adult: Please tell me what time it is.
Child: No.
Adult: But I am late for work and I have to know.
Child: No.

Adult: I have been told that you are really good at taking care of animals. Will you come help me feed some sick kittens I have in the basement?
Child: No.
Adult: If you don't help me, the kittens are going to die.
Child: No.

Adult: Your mother is sick and told me to pick you up. Get in the car and I'll take you home.
Child: No.
Adult: If you don't listen to me, your mother is going to be mad at you. Get in the car.
Child: No.

Playing this game usually brings up many feelings in both the adults and children. This is the purpose of the exercise. These feelings should be discussed. This game can be explained to children in the following way: "Sometimes saying no can be uncomfortable and frightening. It is important to practice it, despite these feelings, so that if you ever need to say no to protect yourself or because you have a funny feeling that what an adult is asking you to do is wrong, you will be able to do so." How a child can apply assertiveness techniques to specific situations will be explained in the following chapter.

The Right to Lie and Not Answer Questions

Children are usually taught that lying is wrong. However, we as adults know that lying is a useful social skill and personal safety strategy. Children need to be told that it is all right for them to lie in order to protect themselves from harm and that they don't have to answer questions an adult asks. In the following exercise the child has been instructed never to say he is alone in the house:

(Phone rings)
Adult: Hello, can I talk to your father?
Child: Daddy's in the shower. Can I take a message and he will call you back soon?
Adult: When will he be done? It is important!
Child: Who's calling please?
Adult: It doesn't matter, just get your father to the phone!
Child: You'll either have to call back later or leave a message.

In this case the child, alone in the house, lied in order to comply with his parents' rule. The child knows that his parents will back him up for doing this, even if the caller turns out to be a friend. In other cases a child can be told, "If someone asks you to go somewhere and you don't want to go, you can say, 'My mother doesn't let me go without her' or 'That's against my father's rules,' even if that's not true."

The Right to Refuse Gifts

A common strategy for child molesters is to offer a child some kind of gift or favor in exchange for submission. Just as with touch or affection, many gifts are signs of love, but a child does not have to unconditionally accept them and certainly doesn't have to accept any terms that go with them. The child should not be made to feel guilty for refusing a present: "Sometimes people try to trick you into doing something that you won't want to do by offering you a present. They may offer you money or food, or they may say they will take you somewhere that you want to go. If anyone offers you favors, you can say that you have to check with me first."

For older children, who will not want to check with a parent, other strategies can be applied: "If someone is pressuring you to accept their gift or favor, it's OK to say, 'I'm sorry, but I'm not hungry/am going home now/don't need money/don't want to go to the park/am not interested in modeling jobs/will come back later with a friend.' If the person gets annoyed, it probably means that they don't have your best interest at heart. If you do accept a gift, it doesn't mean you are obligated to that person. They have no right to demand that you do anything in exchange. A gift should be free of obligation."

The Right to Be Rude or Unhelpful

Child attackers will often rely on the child's desire to be helpful in order to gain access to the child. Sometimes it is necessary to be rude in order to maintain one's safety. The following illustrates how to reinforce this right: "If you ever get lost or separated from me while we are shopping, I want you to go to a cashier for help. If someone who is not a worker in the store offers to help you, you can either say no, thank you or ask them to get a cashier and come back to you. This may feel like you are being rude or not nice when someone is trying to help you, but that way I'll be sure that you'll get someone to help you who will know how to find me." It can be explained to children that the worst that will happen in situations such as these is that they will hurt someone's feelings but that hurting someone's feelings is not as important as protecting their safety.

Children have to understand that personal safety sometimes involves doing things that are ordinarily considered rude. For many children this often involves not giving directions when asked on the street or refusing to open the door while babysitting or when home alone or refusing to respond to an adult's request for assistance. For example, an attacker may knock on the door stating he's been in an accident and needs to use the phone.

The child home alone can offer to make the call for him, call a neighbor, or call the police. It can be explained to children that there are ways to help without putting themselves in jeopardy and that they are not under obligation to assist every adult that asks for their help.

The Right to Run, Scream, and Make a Scene

Attackers often rely on a child's compliance. Sometimes a loud yell will startle an attacker, or causing a scene (crying, kicking, attempts at running away, etc.) will alert others that something is wrong. It is helpful to practice with children the kinds of things that they can yell: "My mother doesn't want me to go with you"; "Get help, this man (or woman) is trying to take me away"; "Leave me alone"; "I won't let you do this to me." We will explain this in greater detail in the following chapter.

The Right to Bite, Hit, and Kick

In some cases a child's safest option may be physical resistance. Children are natural fighters and can be taught to focus on vulnerable areas: kicking knees and shins, poking into the throat or biting. Children can also be taught how to use their size, speed and environment to their advantage. These strategies can enable a child to stun or distract an attacker, giving the child time to run away safely. An in-depth explanation of these strategies will be given in the following chapter.

The Right to Ask for Help

It is important for children to understand their right to get help if something happens to them. What-if games can be played to teach them how to do this. For example, "What if something happened and you were afraid to tell me? Who would you go to for help?" Storytelling is also an effective teaching tool. For example, "I heard a story about a little boy who was being bothered by his daddy's friend, and he was afraid to tell his daddy. He knew he had to get help, so he asked his teacher what to do." It is also a good idea to teach children the names and numbers of people they can call for help, as well as giving them instructions for calling the police.

*   *   *

This chapter has covered the concrete information needed to begin to talk to children about personal-safety issues. This information enables us to overcome the communication barriers mentioned earlier and at the same time impart personal-safety information in a nonthreatening manner. Thus, we can make it possible for children to effectively deal with their personal safety. The next step is teaching children specific crime-prevention and self-defense strategies.

6

Self-Defense

When I was a child I watched my father teach my younger brother how to fight so he could handle the bullies at school. I asked my father to teach me also, and he refused. When I was twelve a neighbor was teaching the local kids judo. I asked him if I could join the classes. He told me to come over for an interview. He sat me down and explained that he didn't teach girls because they would use the skills unwisely. I didn't even understand what he was talking about. I've often wondered how different my adolescence would have been if I had known how to defend myself.

Teaching children self-defense challenges all our beliefs about their strength, our power over them, and our ability and desire to control their behavior. When the subject of teaching self-defense to children is raised most adults have a range of reactions. Some common responses include:

I am raising my son to be peaceful and nonviolent. I don't want him to learn to be aggressive.

It's fine for boys to learn, but it's not a good idea for girls.

My son is already getting into fights at school. Self-defense training would only make things worse.

If I teach my daughter self-defense how do I control
when and how she uses the skills? What if she uses the
techniques on her friends or siblings or on me?

Teaching children would only give them false confidence. If they ever tried to use it, they would anger the
attacker and endanger their safety.

Girls need it, but boys don't. They are naturally aggressive.

I've watched the kids at the local karate school. They
act like little soldiers. I don't want my child to look like
that.

What could a child possibly do to hurt an adult?

Self-defense is anything that enables someone to safely escape a dangerous situation. It can be crossing the street if being
followed; not answering questions over the telephone; refusing
to open the door to a stranger; saying no; screaming and yelling;
making a scene; calling for help; running away; talking calmly
to an attacker; cooperating with an attacker or physically re-
sisting an assault. Self-defense is not just kick and punch. It
is not the application of wartime strategies to everyday life. It
is a state of mind and body that allows one to feel comfortable
in relation to one's safety. It is the belief that one's own personal
safety is more important than the temporary discomfort of an
assailant—no matter who the assailant is. Self-defense is the
knowledge that one's physical and emotional well-being is in
one's own control and is not controlled by others.

Children, as well as adults, have many misconceptions of
what self-defense is. Since children naturally identify with animals, we have found the following explanation useful when
explaining self-defense to children:

Pretend I brought a raccoon in here right now. Pretend
this book is a trap. The raccoon would walk around it.
If I set up a pathway where it had no choice but to walk
in the direction of the trap, the raccoon would probably
stop at the beginning of the pathway. If I started poking
it and it had to keep going, it would stop when it got to

the trap. If I poked again and it had to step into the trap, it would but only by being forced. It is not because the raccoon necessarily knows that the trap is dangerous; it just senses it. The raccoon would sense that something was wrong. After getting caught in the trap, do you know what raccoons do? They bite off the foot that is caught in order to get away. They know that if they stay someone is going to come and kill them. At that point they make the decision that they are better off getting away with three feet than staying in the trap with four and getting killed. People are the same way. We all make decisions on that level. We don't want to die so we make decisions that will make us safer. Sometimes it means doing things that we don't want to do or doing things that hurt us, but we are trying to save our lives. That is what is important. We take self-defense so that we will know more about what is dangerous and how to get away.

Personal-safety strategies can be presented in the same manner in which fire and traffic safety is approached. Children know why they have to "cross on the green and not in between," but children often don't understand why they are told not to ride in an elevator alone or not to hitchhike or not to walk to the local store by themselves. Some parents begin by explaining as much as possible why they are setting up certain rules: "When my daughter was three my rule was that if we were outside, for instance in the playground or shopping, she always had to be where I could see her. I told her that the rule was to make sure that she didn't get lost or hurt and that if something happened to upset her she would know where to find me."

One kindergarten teacher, herself trained in self-defense, used the following means to bring up the subject with her class: "I was reading them 'Little Red Riding Hood.' When I got to the part where the wolf starts chasing her, I changed the story. I had Little Red Riding Hood hit the wolf in the nose and run away. The children loved it. Then I asked them, 'If someone was following you, what would you do?'"

Some adults begin discussing specific safety strategies with children after a child has heard about or read of a crime incident. Crime is a subject that usually comes up at some point in every home and school environment. What-if games, fantasies, telling stories from one's own childhood, or asking advice about another child are good ways to ascertain the child's current knowledge and help him or her start discussing the subject. A third-grade teacher used the strategy of asking advice about another child when her students started asking questions about being bothered on the way home from school: "I know a little girl who has a problem. Every time she goes home the doorman in her building tries to make her give him a kiss. It makes her feel funny and she doesn't like it. What do you think she could do?" The children responded with solutions ranging from the fantastical to the practical:

Why doesn't she tell her parents?

Why doesn't she leave her house by tying a rope from the window and climbing down so she doesn't have to go past him?

She could ask her parents to tell him to leave her alone.

She could dress up like a boy so he won't bother her.

Answers such as these reflect a child's current awareness and give clues as to how to talk to him or her. For example, the child who suggested that the little girl dress up like a boy could be asked, "Do little boys ever get kissed when they don't want to be?" The child can then be given accurate information: "In fact, little boys get bothered like that just as much as little girls do."

What-if games are good ways to teach children what kinds of ploys might be used against them and to increase their awareness:

Adult: What if you are walking to school and a car drives up and the man or woman inside asks for directions, what can you do?
Child: Answer at a distance in a loud voice.
Adult: That's a good answer. Is it a good idea to go near the car?
Child: No.
Adult: Why not?
Child: Because they may try to grab you or rob you.

Adult: What if you came out of school and a man who looked slightly familiar came up to you and said he was your father's friend, that your mother was in the hospital, and that your father had sent him to drive you to the hospital?

Child: I wouldn't go.

Adult: What if you got scared and thought that your mother was really sick?

Child: I'd call home first and see if it was true or I'd go back into school and ask my teacher what to do, because my mother always told me that if anything happened she would tell Grandpa or Aunt Jane to pick me up.

Creating fantasies is also a good way for children to figure out how to handle scary situations. With fantasies the actual situations may not be realistic, but children's sense of their own power and ability to protect themselves is what is important. One child, who had been struggling with her fears about being Jewish and dealing with anti-Semitism, had the following fantasy after her second self-defense class: "I was walking home and suddenly I saw this Nazi parade. I was wearing my Star of David around my neck, so they could see I was Jewish. One Nazi came over to me and started to attack me. He kept saying he didn't like Jews. I remembered what you taught us and I started to yell, 'Leave me alone, get off me, get away.' He was really surprised and he ran away."

What-if games, role playing, fantasies, reworking fairy tales and telling incidents from our own childhoods are ways of presenting safety strategies that allow the children to think by themselves and feel in control of safety regulations. It is important when developing these strategies to stress the positive and not put down the child's answers. If a child's safety strategy does not feel comfortable to us it is better to say, "That's one good way, what could be another?" rather than to say, "That's not smart, I don't want you handling it that way." A positive, noncritical approach improves the child's chances of following the safety tips and also develops their facility for spontaneous problem solving in unexpected situations.

As children reach adolescence, different strategies need to be developed. Adolescence is a time when most children feel a need for independence, particularly from parental rules and regulations. Adolescents want to expand their options and will often test and challenge authority. They will also turn more often to peers rather than to adults for advice, guidance, and behavior models. In addition, because they are developing sexually and becoming more aware of themselves and others as sexual beings, the issue of sexual assault is especially confusing. Sexual assault and personal safety may be subjects that terrify them, but they often feel the need to act as if the issues were silly and parental worry unnecessary. In our experience, adolescents who have a history of being sexually assaulted earlier in their childhoods find themselves confronted with their unresolved feelings.

I was attacked when I was nine. I never told anyone. I pushed it out of my thoughts and never really dealt with my feelings about it. I had been out when I wasn't supposed to be and always blamed myself for being stupid. When I was fourteen I suddenly realized that I was terrified of boys and men. I didn't want to have to deal with the attack or tell anybody, but I didn't know what to do with the fear or how to explain it. At a time when everyone else was dating I avoided it at all costs. I became a bookworm, a babysitter; I tutored other students and basically did everything I could to avoid dealing with dating. I felt very alone and crazy throughout my adolescence. Some people suspected something was wrong, but nobody asked me.

It is crucial at this time to keep communication lines as open as possible in order to protect the child. Parents, guardians, teachers, and professionals all have different ideas about teenagers staying out late, dating, engaging in sexual activity, and challenging authority. For the sake of the child's well-being it becomes especially important to discuss the subject of personal safety in a nonjudgmental, direct, and open manner.

One mother explained her concerns in the following way:

When my daughter reached fourteen I became frantic. I had been raped when I was fourteen and had never really dealt with it. I didn't want my daughter to get hurt, but I knew that if I became too protective she would just sneak out. One day I took a deep breath and told her what had happened to me. I told her how scared I had been, how I couldn't tell my mother, how I had always blamed myself, and how frightened I was for her.

I told her that part of the process of her growing up and becoming more independent was that she would be breaking some of my rules. Then I told her that there were more dangers than I could possibly protect her from but that no matter what rule she had broken she could call me anytime of the day or night from anywhere and I would be there.

Another woman recounted the way her father handled her becoming an adolescent:

> When I was fifteen my father told me that if I went out and stayed out late and was worried for any reason about coming home that I could call him and he would come pick me up, no questions asked. He also told me that he trusted my integrity and hoped that I would call him when I needed to.

In one small town, where drunk drivers were becoming an increasing problem, the adolescents made a formal pact with their parents. The agreement was that if a teenager felt incapable of driving home at any time, he or she could call home and a parent would pick them up. Part of the agreement was that there would be no questions asked and no arguments later. Accidents as a result of drunk driving decreased dramatically within a few months. In both of these situations the safety of children was given priority so that open communication and effective planning were possible.

Every child has different safety problem areas in his or her daily life. Children can be asked at what points in their routines they feel afraid, and strategies can then be worked out. The following are some examples of common safety problem areas and ways of evaluating and handling them:

BEING FOLLOWED

If a child suspects he or she is being followed on the way to school or coming home from the local store, for example, the first step is for the child to trust his/her instinct. A child will want to think, "I am just imagining this" or, "If I don't think about it, it will go away" or, "If I just hurry home I will be OK." The reality is that if the situation is ignored, the attacker has the chance to move in and take the child by surprise. It is always better to know what one is up against. In the case of being followed there are several ways of ascertaining this. One way is to simply turn around and look. Children on a city or town street can use shop windows as mirrors to see who is behind them. Once the child sees who is directly behind, he or she can decide how to handle it.

One nine-year-old girl related averting potential danger in the following way:

> I was walking home from school, and I thought this man was following me. I had seen him in the neighborhood before, and he always gave me a creepy feeling. I crossed the street, and he crossed behind me. Then I got scared. I ran into my church and called my mother and waited there until she came and picked me up.

A ten-year-old boy used the following imaginative strategy when he realized a teenager was following him after having seen him put money in his pocket:

> I knew he had seen that I had some money and that he was going to rob me. I went into a store and told the shopkeeper about it. I told him that I wanted to give him my money and buy a really cheap item that the teenager wouldn't want to steal. I said that if he stopped following me I would come back and return the item. I bought this really cheap thing and came out of the store with it. The teenager saw it and stopped following me. My plan was that if it hadn't worked I was going to go back into the store and call the police.

As the above situations indicate, it is important for children at a young age to be familiarized with their neighborhoods. They need to know what stores are open and at what hours. Adults can point out different ones in different areas as places children can run to if they are ever in trouble. In many communities there are restaurants, stores, and homes that have been designated as "Safe Havens." These are places where the owners or occupants have agreed to help children in trouble. They are sometimes designated by special stickers. In some neighborhoods the police or community members take children on neighborhood field trips in order for them to learn where the Safe Havens are, what streets are particularly dangerous to cross, and other safety information.

If a child is being followed in a semipublic area, one strategy is for the child to yell, "Mommy, wait for me," and/or run to a crowded area. Children need to be told that it is OK to lie and act as if Mommy or Daddy or their friend is right up the block, even if they are not. A child being followed on the way home has a number of options depending on where they live and whether or not someone will be home when they get there. They can change their route and not go home, go to a neighbor's home, go to a store, or call their parents for assistance. It is helpful for children to know their neighbors' schedules and phone numbers. In an apartment building parents can set up strategies with other tenants so that if a child is followed into the lobby, the child can buzz the neighbor's bell with a signal that indicates trouble (three short rings, for example). The neighbor can then investigate or call the police. Children followed into their lobbies can also pretend that they don't live in the building and are just visiting a friend or relative they are going to wait for downstairs.

For rural children or children being followed in a deserted area, running into a crowd, calling for Mommy, or going into a store are often not options. Since children are natural explorers, they will often be more familiar with their environment than adults will be. This inclination to explore can be utilized for safety purposes. Children can be encouraged to know where streams or trails lead and where good hiding places are. They can be alerted to objects in their environment, such as sticks and rocks, that can be used to protect them. In rural areas children are often followed by people in cars. If that happens the child can get off the road, run into the woods, follow a trail or stream, hide behind a rock, or climb a tree. Attackers will seldom leave their cars unattended to follow a child and, as previously stated, will be less familiar with the surroundings. Most importantly, the child must keep as great a distance as possible from the attacker. Some families set up codes to use if a child is lost or in trouble, such as a certain whistle. If the child needs help, they keep whistling the code until they hear a response.

AT HOME

Safety strategies for the problems children confront at home will depend on the child's age and the specific situation. It is important for children to know all the different exits in their homes and how to use the phone to get help. Using the phone is also important for teaching fire safety and what to do if an adult gets sick or is injured. Children as young as three can be taught to dial emergency phone numbers and ask for help. Some families keep emergency numbers near the phone, and others put stickers on the phone. It is important to practice making an emergency call with the child, having the child state his or her name, address, phone number, and the nature of the emergency. The phone company has booklets specifically designed to teach children how to use the phone in case of emergency. Children can also be instructed where and to whom to run for help: "If Mommy is ever sick, go tell Mrs. Jones next door, and she will be able to get help for us."

If an assault, which is primarily directed against an adult, begins in the home, often the best strategy for the child will be to leave and get help. One father reported the following:

> Burglars broke into our home one night. They tied me and my two oldest children to chairs. My youngest son was only four, and they didn't bother with him. When he realized what was happening, he climbed out a window and went to a neighbor's for help. They called the police, and the burglars were apprehended while they were going through the closets upstairs. None of us were hurt.

Some attackers will try to intimidate adults by threatening their children's safety. In these cases the family can maintain their safety by working as a team. Some parents teach their children code words that indicate danger. Such code words can be particularly important for situations where an adult is in danger from an acquaintance, and the child is not sure if something is wrong. One mother used this technique successfully:

> When I was little my mother was attacked in our home, and I didn't know what to do or how to get help.

I was always afraid that something like that could happen to my daughter and myself. I developed a code with her. I told her that if I ever felt endangered in our home I would tell her to go into her room and play with her rabbit, and that would mean she was to go to the phone and call the police for help. One night a neighbor came over and began threatening me. He started screaming, and my daughter woke up. When she came out into the living room to see what was wrong, I told her to go back into her room and play with her rabbit. She remembered our code and called the police. They came before I was hurt.

Sometimes children are told by the attacker to be quiet or to go into their rooms or participate in or witness the assault on a parent:

I was at home with my thirteen-year-old daughter when a man broke in. He told my daughter to go into her room and close the door. She did so. He pushed me into my room and began tearing at my clothes. We live in a farmhouse and are far away from any help. My daughter came up behind him and hit him over the head with a heavy vase. He was knocked unconscious, and we were able to call the police.

Attackers will expect the child to comply with their demands and will often be startled if the child resists in any way:

In the middle of the night a man entered through my bedroom window. He pinned me down and began beating me over the head with a hammer. My four-year-old daughter woke up and heard him. She ran into my room and started screaming, "Go away, stop hurting my mommy." She just wouldn't stop, and the man ran away. Neighbors were alerted by her screams and called the police. The man was apprehended. I was badly hurt, but I feel my daughter saved me from being killed.

Children left by themselves at home need to think primarily of getting out of the house or getting help. Cooperating with or immobilizing the assailant may be options, depending on the circumstances. As with every situation, it is important for the child or children to trust their instincts:

> My friend and I were fourteen and were babysitting for an infant. Two local teenagers, whom we vaguely knew, saw us through the window and started banging on the door, demanding to be let in. We refused. They started yelling at us. They began to open a window. The phone was right next to the window. I was scared, but I went to the phone anyway and called my father. As soon as they saw me pick up the phone, they ran away.

In this case one girl had an agreement with her father that if she needed help she could call him. It is important when children and adolescents are going to be alone that they know whom they can call in an emergency. In addition, strategies as to how they can work together can be discussed so that when they find themselves in such a situation they can effectively use team approaches.

ELEVATORS

Elevators, which are confined spaces with only one escape route, are danger spots for everyone but especially for children. Attackers operate in several ways in elevators. One way is to get in the elevator with the intended victim, press the STOP button, and carry out an assault between floors. Another is to take the elevator to the basement or roof and assault the person there. A third pattern is for the attacker to wait in the basement and call the elevator when he hears someone entering on the lobby floor. The elevator will take the unsuspecting passenger down, and the assault will take place in the basement.

The first step for safety is to view elevators from the perspective of whether the child is tall enough to reach the control panel. Children who cannot reach the controls are not safe riding without a trusted adult. Children who are able to reach the control panel can be told to stand near it when they ride in the elevator, thereby limiting the attacker's access to the STOP button. If an incident begins in an elevator, a good strategy for the child is to press as many buttons as possible. This way the elevator will open at another floor quickly, and the child can get away. Children entering on the lobby level should make sure the elevator is on its way up. If they are not sure, they can send the elevator down to the basement first and enter it when it comes back up.

It is important for children to know that they do not have to get on the elevator if they feel uncomfortable about someone who is also getting on. They can say, "Go on ahead, I'm waiting for my father/mother/friend" or "Oh, I forgot something, don't wait for me." If a child is on an elevator and gets a funny feeling that something is wrong, he or she can press the button and get off at the next floor.

We have explored only a few of the situations in which children may be at risk. What is most important is to alert children to potential dangers and help them develop practical safety measures. It is also important to allow children to share stories of times they have used various strategies and to praise them for putting safety techniques to good use. One school had an extensive safety-training campaign. A student was walking to school when a man pulled up in a car and told her to get in. As she had been taught, she screamed NO and ran away. She told the principal and was presented with an award. The more children are rewarded for using safety tips, the more they will use them and the more capable they will be of protecting themselves.

SELF-PROTECTION TECHNIQUES

Despite a child's best precautionary efforts, sometimes assault is unavoidable. In such circumstances it is important to remember that it is not the child's fault. It is also crucial to reassure the child that he or she did nothing wrong. When faced with assault, children have a range of options from complete cooperation to physical resistance. The strategy the child uses will depend on the child's instincts in the situation, who the attacker is, where the attack is taking place, what kind of force or coercion is being used, and what kind of training in self-protection the child has had. When teaching self-defense to children, it must be stressed that there are no rules and no magic answers. Each child will have to trust his or her instincts and do the best possible in any given situation. They should not be told that they have to fight or be considered sissy or that if they don't cooperate they will get themselves killed. Children need to be told that they have good instincts and that it is their choice, and their choice alone, how to handle a potential assault.

Traditionally, people have been told to beg, plead, burst into tears, fake an asthma attack, vomit, tell an attacker they are sick—anything that would either repulse the attacker or make him or her feel sorry for the victim. If we examine the motivations of the child molester, however, we can see that these strategies are not likely to be effective. Attackers pick on children because they are usually easy to control, because they want to hurt children, and because they see children as helpless and vulnerable. Pleading for mercy and bursting into tears are often the exact responses the offender is looking for. The strategy of trying to make oneself repulsive by vomiting or urinating is based on the false premise that sexual assault is a sexually motivated crime. Though all of these strategies have worked for someone at some time, they are statistically the least effective of defenses. Calm, direct, verbal communication from a child will startle many child molesters. Startling the attacker can sometimes stop the attack and enable the child to buy time and get away. The following examples illustrate different types of successful verbal strategies:

A seven-year-old girl was learning how to rollerskate. She was concentrating intensely on her feet and didn't realize that she had become separated from her friends. A man picked her up and carried her into an alleyway. She said to him, "Mister, I'll do what you want if you put me down." He put her down, whereupon she screamed, "This man is trying to take me away," and skated out of the alley as fast as she could. People were alerted by her cries, came running, and caught the man. He was arrested, and it was discovered that he was wanted in several cases of child molestation.

An eight-year-old girl was abducted in a car. Her kidnapper was driving her along a highway. She told him that she had to go to the bathroom, and he stopped at a gas station. He accompanied her to the bathroom door and told her he would wait outside. She locked herself in the bathroom and refused to come out. The man attempted to break the lock, and the gas station attendant came to see what was wrong. The child screamed, "That man is not my daddy; call my mommy," and gave the attendant her phone number. While her mother was being called the abductor escaped. The girl was taken home safely.

A fourteen-year-old boy noticed that a man was following him around in a department store. He assumed at first that the man was a security guard. Then the man came up to him and said in a threatening tone, "I have my eye on you, and I'd really like to get you. I like your body. I am going to follow you out of here and see where you go." The boy said, "You don't have to do that, why don't we go in there?" He gestured toward the men's room and added, "I'll meet you in there." As the man entered the men's room, the boy ran away.

In the above examples, children used strategies that were extensions of the assertiveness skills and children's bill of personal safety rights outlined in Chapter Four. In all the instances cited the attackers were confident of the child's compliance. The children lied in order to protect themselves. In the first two examples the children screamed and made a scene and were able to alert others to the situation. As these examples illustrate, tricks natural to children are often effective safety strategies. Role-plays can be used to help children think about these kinds of situations and to allow them to practice specific ways to say no to adult demands or lie in order to protect themselves. For example, a common pattern of attack in rural areas is for a child molester to tell a child that he has found a sick animal or something else exciting in the woods as a way of enticing the child to go with him. The following role-play can be acted out:

Adult: Guess what, I just found a baby deer in a cave. It was just born and I'm sure it hasn't run away yet. Do you want to come and see it? The mother knows me because I have been visiting it. She'll let you come visit the baby, if you come with me.

Child: Tell me where the cave is. I'm on my way to visit

my friends and I'll go visit the deer later.

Adult: I don't know how long she is going to stay there. You're going to miss it if you don't come right away.

Child: I've seen lots of deer. If I miss it, I'll see another some other time.

When role-playing it is important to let children try different strategies and different kinds of cons, ranging from bribes to threats. Children need to develop strategies that allow them to "save face."

In situations where children are being sexually abused by someone living in their home or by someone who visits often, there are a variety of options. Some include the child trying to stop the abuse alone or telling someone else in order to get help. Issues of disclosure and what an adult should do if a child reveals such abuse will be explored in Chapters Eight and Nine. Though these situations are complicated and in some ways the hardest for children to defend against, many children have managed to stop an assault using assertiveness strategies. For example, a sixteen-year-old girl with a history of being sexually abused by her father began therapy. After several sessions of working on assertiveness techniques she related the following: "What my father would do is sneak into my room in the middle of the night to molest me. For years, I just pretended to be asleep and told myself it wasn't happening. The other night, when I heard the doorknob turn, I said in a loud voice, 'Daddy, I'm up, what do you want?' He didn't come in that night." The girl was so encouraged by this that she continued in therapy and later managed to get her family to come in for help.

When I was eight, my uncle visited us. At one point we were alone in a room together, though there were other people in other parts of the house. He started to molest me. I started to cry and told him I would tell my mother. He didn't stop so I started yelling, "I am going to tell!" He was afraid people would hear me and stopped. He never bothered me again and he told me he was sorry.

In some situations, calm verbal communication is not enough, and then yelling and screaming are often good strategies. Yelling has several purposes. The first is to mobilize the child's spirit and help the child overcome the "freezing" or panic response that so often is the first reaction during an assault. Many children will hold their breath when they are frightened. If they are yelling, they will automatically keep breathing. Yelling helps the child translate fear into anger, and helplessness into power.

Children are often discouraged from having loud voices and are told to be quiet or to "shut-up" if they begin to scream, cry, or make a lot of noise. By the time we are adults, many of us have lost the ability to yell when we are threatened. Many adults and children report having nightmares in which they are attacked, and when they open their mouths to scream, nothing comes out but a whisper. Instead of uniformly telling children to be quiet, we can learn to appreciate the power of their voices, recognizing that this power can enable them to protect themselves when in danger. We can teach them when it is, and isn't, appropriate to yell.

My six-year-old daughter has been taking self-defense lessons for a year. She loves to scream. Instead of just telling her to stop or punishing her, I now tell her that she has a really good scream, but I don't want her to use it in the house unless she is in danger.

Yelling is a skill that can be learned and practiced. The more children practice and are encouraged, the more confident they will feel, and the easier it will be for them to yell when they are in a dangerous situation. A loud yell comes from the diaphragm. In order to breathe properly, the child must relax the throat. Children can be taught in the following way: "Put your hands on your stomach. Take a deep breath and feel your stomach expand like a balloon. Blow the breath out and feel your stomach deflate, like a balloon losing its air." After children can feel their breathing and are breathing deeply, the next step is to let them yell as loudly as they can on the exhale. They can yell a sound or a word. Children commonly like to yell: "No," "Stop it," "Creep," "Get away," "Get off," "I hate you," "I won't," "Mommy," "Daddy," "Leave me alone."

A good way to practice is for a child to yell into a pillow. This way the sound won't disturb anyone. The child can be told to yell whatever they want at whomever they want, for as long as they want. It is important to tell them that yelling may make them feel angry and that that is OK. While they are yelling they can also pound a mattress or another pillow. It is crucial for the child to feel completely in control. Therefore, it is imperative that they hold the pillow themselves. This exercise is useful in teaching safety, as well as a good way of releasing aggression.

The following games are ways of teaching yelling to groups of children:

CIRCLE OF SPIRIT

The children form a circle while holding hands and closing their eyes. They are instructed to take a deep breath and find in themselves the part of them that is most powerful. They are told to yell a sound or a word that expresses how strong they are. The sound can be as scary or as weird as they want it to be. The leader yells first, squeezes the hand of the next child who yells second, and so on. The more times the circle is repeated, the stronger the yells will become. We have found that some children yell out the name of someone who has hurt them or develop sounds like a tiger growling in the jungle. This exercise frees children to think of themselves as powerful and tells them that it is all right to be able to scare somebody. It also helps them realize how loud they each can be and how powerful yelling can be. To accentuate this point, this game can be ended with all the children yelling together.

ECHO GAME

The children form a circle and make fists with their hands. They are instructed to take a deep breath and think about something that makes them angry (being teased or bullied at school, for example). They pound the air with their fists, and, if the surroundings permit, they also stomp on the floor. The leader yells out a word or a sound, and the children echo it back as a group. This helps them yell loudly without feeling self-conscious, since they're doing it in a group. As with the other exercise, it helps them appreciate the strength of each other's voices as well as the strength of their voices together. A variation of this game is for the children to hold hands and jump up and down each time they echo back the leader's yell.

These games and exercises are excellent for self-defense purposes and also enable children to release feelings of fear, anger, and aggression in a safe and constructive manner. Children should never be judged or criticized for their yells during or after these games. They should be told only that they are doing fine and be encouraged to yell louder and harder. It is also important to realize that some children become frightened or upset during these exercises. It should be explained to them that these are normal feelings and nothing to be ashamed of or embarrassed about. Children should never be forced to do exercises that make them feel uncomfortable. However, they can be allowed to observe such exercises with the understanding that when they feel they are ready to try, they can.

In actual assault situations children need to trust their instincts and yell whatever seems appropriate. Unfortunately, in some situations, yelling FIRE will more likely bring aid than yelling for help. In a public area, yelling MOMMY or THIS MAN IS NOT MY FATHER can be effective ways for children to alert other adults to their situation. In totally deserted areas, yelling is not likely to bring aid, but it can be a useful tool to help children overcome fear and think more clearly.

COOPERATION

In some situations the safest option may be for the child to cooperate. A good example is a robbery attempt. Children should be told to surrender property rather than risk getting hurt. Be sure to spell this out clearly; children often feel that they have to fight for something that is valuable to their parents or that was given to them by their parents. When confronted by a mugger, particularly one with a weapon, the child must remain calm and project a confident attitude. The following is an example of cooperation in the course of a robbery.

Assailant: Shut up and you won't get hurt.
Child: OK.
Assailant: Give me all your money.
Child: My money is in my knapsack. I'll get it for you.

[The child moves slowly, indicating that he or she is not planning to fight, and hands over the money.] This is all I have.
   Assailant: Give me your watch.
   Child: OK.
   Assailant: Turn around and don't look back and count to 100.
   Child: OK. 1, 2, 3 . . .

In order to control fear, the child can take a deep breath. It is essential to speak in a calm, soft voice and to try not to express fear, hostility, anger, or resentment. If the child has money hidden somewhere, such as in a shoe, the assailant should be informed. It is not worth risking being searched and having the assailant discover that the child was trying to hold out. While cooperating, the child needs to remain alert in case the situation escalates to bodily assault. It is important to remember that while cooperation is often the best strategy initially, it does not guarantee that a physical assault will not occur.

PHYSICAL RESISTANCE

In some situations verbal defenses, cooperation, or running away may not be viable or effective options. Even though we may be uncomfortable with the thought of teaching children physical resistance, we have to remember that there are times when such skills can save a child's life. A child faced with kidnapping, beating, sexual molestation, or murder may find that physical resistance is the only way to survive.

I was always adamantly opposed to girls learning self-defense. I thought it was unfeminine and unhealthy. Then I read in the paper about a sixteen-year-old girl who was confronted by a rapist with a knife. He took her into an alley and raped her. She cooperated totally with his demands, and after it was over he was going to kill her anyway. When she saw the knife coming toward her she realized she was about to die. She put her hand up, got the knife away from him, and stabbed him. I realized that she could have been my daughter or anyone else's for that matter. I had always believed that if you just

cooperated with an attacker you'd be safe. Until I read
that account it didn't occur to me that they might decide
to kill you anyway. I realized that my concern about my
daughter's femininity was actually leaving my daughter
defenseless.

Just as children can role-play, fantasize, and practice crime-
prevention and assertiveness strategies, they can use these techniques to acquire self-defense skills. Traditionally, parents,
usually fathers, teach their children, especially boys, how to
fight. Children often play-fight with each other, wrestle, have
pillow fights, and act out exciting spy or war scenarios they
have seen on TV or read about. These common types of play
can be adapted and utilized for teaching children practical self-
protection. Whether or not we have access to supportive self-
defense classes for children, parents, teachers, and guardians
can incorporate many of the principles and exercises outlined
when playing with and teaching children.
One first-grade teacher related the following:

When it came time to play Simon Says I started incorporating self-defense strategies. When I was Simon,
I would say, "Simon says, say NO"; "Simon says, yell";
"Simon says, do a palm heel"; "Simon says, throw a
punch." After a while the children became proficient with
the techniques, and they took turns being Simon. After
each game we would usually have a discussion about
crime prevention and self-protection.

Many of us have misconceptions about what effective resistance is. Some of us believe that if we hit an assailant he
or she will become angry and kill us; others think there is
nothing we can do to hurt an assailant. In reality, attackers are
expecting victims, not opponents. Effective physical resistance
from a child will usually come as a complete surprise.
The following examples illustrate how children we've known
have used physical techniques to safely escape danger:

A six-year-old boy was confronted in the schoolyard
by three older children who threatened to beat him up.
He took a fighter's stance, made direct eye contact and
calmly said, "You'd better not bother me." The bullies

replied, "You must be older than we thought," and backed away.

A seven-year-old girl was abducted in a car. She waited until the kidnapper had to slow down for traffic, then she struck him in the eyes with a spearhand to distract him, opened the car door, jumped out, and ran away.

A six-year-old girl was visiting her friend. Her friend's father asked her to accompany him to the woodshed and help him carry wood. Once inside the woodshed, he locked the door and started to molest the little girl. She kicked him in the shins, climbed out the window, and ran home.

A fourteen-year-old girl was waiting for a bus. A man approached, took away the book she was reading, and grabbed her wrist. As he started to pull her away, she hit him with a knifehand on the side of the neck and stomped his foot. When he doubled over, she escaped.

Effective physical resistance means directing one's defenses against the vulnerable areas of the assailant. It does not mean beating on an attacker's chest, trying to wrestle out of a strong hold, or hitting the attacker's arms or legs, as these areas are not that vulnerable to injury. The goal is to stun and distract the attacker, thereby enabling a safe escape. Children can be taught such techniques at a very young age. They have good instincts and can be taught to rely on them as to when it is appropriate to use the techniques.

As we explained at the beginning of this chapter, many adults are concerned about teaching children self-defense. It is our experience that these skills greatly increase children's ability to prevent and stop assaults and to signal for help if they are assaulted.

The practice of the physical and verbal strategies also increases a child's sense of power. As they begin to develop their physical potential, children start to feel in control of their environments. This sense of strength is essential for children to internalize in order to be prepared to avoid and stop assaults. In addition, this training develops children's self-confidence and positive body images. In our classes children who are initially shy become outgoing, and children who are aggressive and acting out become calmer and more centered. These behavior changes affect all aspects of their lives. One ten-year-old boy said, "When I started self-defense I was having a hard time in school. I wasn't doing so well reading. Once I learned some of the self-defense techniques, learning things in school became easier. I guess I thought that if I could learn self-defense, I could learn anything."

The techniques illustrated in the following pictures are the ones we have found to be the easiest to teach children. We have not included breaks from holds or strategies for disarming an attacker as they require in-depth training to be successfully carried out.

Practice the techniques slowly, with concentration on aim and precision. Your child should be encouraged to execute the blows full power on some sort of target or punching bag (pillow, mattress, phone book).

Children can practice different holds with a partner, giving the "caught" child an opportunity to take notice of which vulnerable areas are accessible to them (eyes, nose, throat, groin, shins) and what techniques they could use to escape. Supervised playfighting, particularly with the use of boxing gloves or other protective equipment, allows children to develop reflexes and learn how to get hit without falling apart. In addition, it allows them to learn to avoid blows and react spontaneously.

When teaching and practicing self-defense techniques with children it is crucial to take the attitude (even if you are unsure) that they can defend themselves successfully if they need to. Relate to them as strong human beings. Instead of focusing on what you assume they can't do, let them know they are capable of learning the techniques. Praise each accomplishment, "Your aim is better." "You're hitting harder." "Your techniques are improving." In order to successfully learn these skills, children must have a sense that adults are confident in their capabilities.

ON GUARD!
A photographic guide to self-defense for young people

THE FIGHTER'S STANCE This is the basic stance from which all techniques can be practiced. The child's legs are a shoulder's width apart, knees slightly bent. This position gives the child enough flexibility and good balance to guard against his being pushed to the ground; the hands are up, protecting the face and stomach.
Photos by Gino Colao

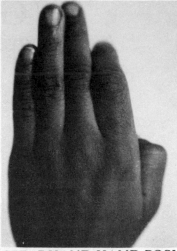

SPEARHAND This technique uses the tips of the fingers to strike toward the eyes or into the hollow of the throat (under the Adam's apple).

SPEARHAND HAND POSITION The wrist is straight, fingers are bent slightly at the tips, and the thumb is tucked out of the way. The hand is kept stiff and firm, so the strike is strong.

Directed into the throat, this technique causes pain and temporary breathing difficulty. Directed toward the eyes, the spearhand is a distraction technique, causing the attacker to automatically protect the eyes by blinking or pulling away. (It will *not* blind the attacker.) This technique can be used close in or at a slight distance in a situation where the attacker is in front of the child and one or both of the child's hands are free.

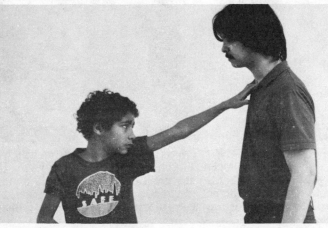

PALM HEEL This technique uses the base, or heel, of the palm to strike into any number of vulnerable areas. It is a close-in technique, used for any frontal attack where one or both of the child's hands are free. Directing the blow up under the nose causes severe pain and disorientation. Striking under the chin or into the stomach or chest doesn't usually cause much pain but can push the attacker back. It can also be directed into the groin, causing pain and possibly nausea.

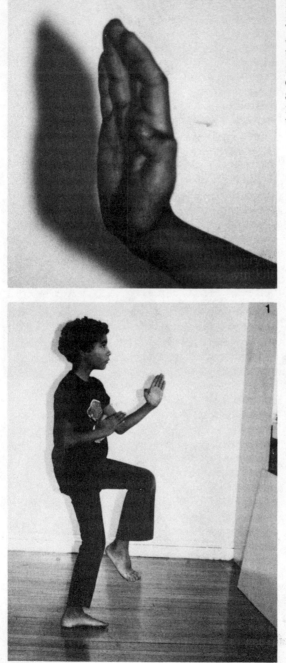

PALM HEEL HAND POSITION The wrist is bent back, the fingers are close together, and the thumb is tucked inside the hand.

FRONT KICK This is one of the simplest and most effective of techniques for children. It is practiced in four steps:

1. The child winds up by lifting the knee and pulling the foot back toward the buttocks. Whether or not the child has shoes on, the toes are pulled up and back, out of the way.

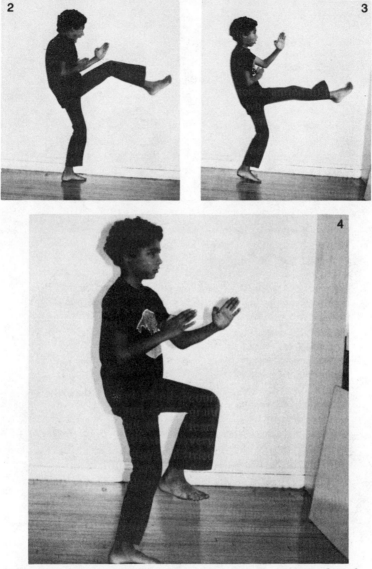

2. The leg extends, with the child using the ball, or heel, of the foot to strike.

3 and 4. The child pulls the foot back to the bent position and then returns to a normal stance. This retraction is important—it not only gives the kick its "snap," making it an extremely effective technique, but it prevents the attacker from grabbing the child's leg.

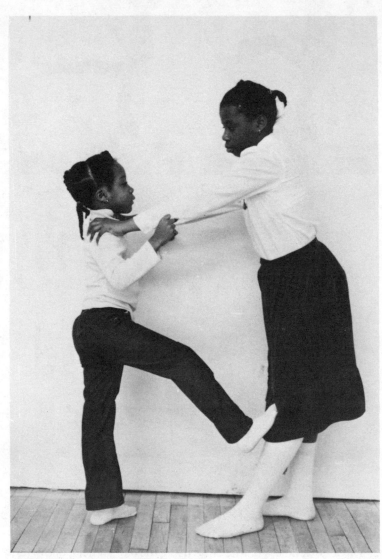

HOW FRONT KICK IS USED The front kick is used in cases of frontal attack, when the attacker is at a slight distance. A strong kick into the knee causes severe pain and possible injury to the knee joint; a kick to the shin is also painful.

INSTEP STOMP This is another simple yet powerful technique that children of almost any age and size can use effectively. The child winds up by picking the knee up high, then slams the heel down on the top of the attacker's foot. The Instep Stomp can also be used if the attacker is behind or to the side of the child. It can provide enough distraction to allow the child to break away and escape; a particularly well-placed thrust can inflict pain to make it difficult for an attacker to pursue.

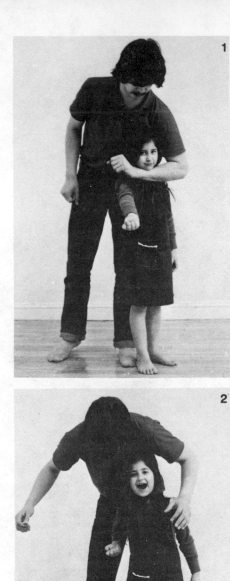

BACK ELBOW Elbow techniques can be used in instances of front, back, and side attacks. This illustrates the back elbow.

1. The child winds up by extending the arm forward, with the hand in a fist.

2. The child bends the arm, directing the point of the elbow straight into the attacker's groin or stomach, depending on the child's size. The elbow should travel straight back, for maximum power.

7

Dealing with Fear

I couldn't breathe and I was afraid that would mean that
I was going to die. That was the worst part of it. Now,
whenever I am scared all of a sudden I can't breathe. I
open my mouth and air just won't come in. Every time
it happens I am afraid that I am going to die. Sometimes
when I get hurt I feel like I am choking, and I don't
know what to do. I don't know how to explain it to
people. They just don't understand.
  —Eight-year-old child who was raped at age six

We live in a world permeated with violent events and in a
society rampant with crime. Violence, be it a large-scale war
or street crime, is presented to us explicitly, through the media.
We can be witness to a frightening event on TV, see pictures
of it and read about it in newspapers and magazines. We not
only read about and see violence close to home, but we are
inundated with information about the violence that occurs
throughout the world. In addition, the entertainment media
reflects this violence. Many movies, TV shows, novels, and
plays contain violence, often portrayed explicitly and with an
underlying sense of hopelessness. When we start to think about
our lives in relation to this violence, we often become overwhelmed with fear and a sense of helplessness. Such fear is a
perfectly normal reaction to the reality around us.

However, we are not really supposed to be afraid. We all
remember messages from our childhoods, "scaredy-cat," "cow-
ard," "yellow-belly," etc. We used these words as ways of
taunting and insulting each other. Now, as adults, our fears

may be termed "childish." If we are men, our fears are called "unmanly." If we are women, we are often called hysterical or paranoid. Consequently, we will often cope with fear by treating it as silly or as an obstacle to correct behavior. We try to pretend it is not there.

Fear is one of the most powerful of emotions. It affects us both physically and psychologically. Fear can be a manifestation of many things: a warning that we are in danger; a warning that a dangerous situation is developing around us; an expression of anger, guilt, despair, or powerlessness; reaction to something that happened in the past.

As adults, we want to minimize our own fears because we are embarrassed by them. We also minimize children's fears. We decide that they have overactive imaginations and are only afraid of things that they make up. Because childhood fears are normal, we decide not to take them seriously. Sometimes we feel that since children do not have to cope with adult problems their fears are not justified.

We have explained strategies for protecting our children and teaching them personal safety. In order to begin to consistently and practically implement these strategies, we must admit to our own and our children's fears and develop ways of handling them.

The first step is take the emotion called fear seriously. It is an emotion as real as grief, guilt, or anger and must be treated as such. As with crime, denial is a strategy that just doesn't work. If we deny children's fears or act as if they are not real, they only become unmanageable. There is nothing as terrifying as being told that your reality is not real, and there is nothing as devastating as being afraid and not having that fear taken seriously.

Last night my little sister was up really late. My father came in and said, "Why aren't you asleep?" She said, "Because I'm scared that a man is going to crawl in the window." He started teasing her, saying, "Oh, there is someone coming in; there is someone at the door." She started crying and kept crying until she fell asleep. I thought my father was being mean, but I was too scared to tell him.

For the child afraid of the monster in the closet, there really is a monster in the closet. It may not be our definition of a monster. It may be a way of asking a question about fear, of getting needed attention from an adult, of expressing anger, of disclosing something that happened, or it may be an expression of a half-remembered incident or nightmare. What is important is the fear itself. Whether or not there is a monster in the closet, the fact remains that the child is afraid. If we are to find out the cause of the fear and help the child manage it, we must take the fear seriously. If we don't, we may never find out what is wrong, and the fear may remain unmanageable into adulthood.

> When I was a child, I was very afraid of the dark. I also didn't need a lot of sleep, which was very unusual for a child. My parents decided that I was creating my fear in order to stay up and read. Staying up reading when you were supposed to be sleeping was bad. They decided that as a compromise they would put a light on in the hall. They reasoned that there would be enough light so I wouldn't be afraid but not enough light for me to read by. They thought it was the perfect solution. However, all it did was create monsters. The light in the hall created shadows. I ended up staying up for hours each night trying to figure out if the shadow was my coat, the closet door, or really a monster. Now, as an adult, I still don't sleep, and I am still afraid of the dark.

For children, fear often takes on magical qualities and is expressed through fantasies and magical beings. For children who are brought up to believe that there are bad people and good people and are told not to talk to strangers, without being given an explanation, creating a monster may be their only way of expressing fear. A monster or bogeyman is often the child's translation of adults' warnings about bad people and strangers. It is ironic that after instilling this fear in them, we turn around and say, "Don't be silly, there is no such thing as a bogeyman."

Children express their fears in a variety of ways. We may not be sure what the causes are or whether something is seriously wrong. Children express fears through nightmares, night terrors, or insomnia. They may have phobias about school or being left alone or an intense fear of the dark. They may exhibit startled responses to noise or touch. Some children are terrified by a particular movie or a scene in a movie, of a certain picture or book, or they become obsessed with a news event they have heard about. Some children's fears are expressed through joking or making fun of violent situations. Often they express their fears through play and games. It is important to learn how to listen to children's fears and help them as well as ourselves understand the causes and manage the symptoms.

My ten-year-old son was waking up every night with nightmares. One night I just told him to go back to sleep, that nothing was wrong, that nothing was going to happen, and that he was safe. I felt like somehow I had squelched his feelings, but I wasn't sure how. I asked a friend about it who said, "Why don't you tell him that if anything does happen, you will come and help him. Telling him nothing is going to happen feels like a lie. You can't guarantee that he is going to be safe."

Since our children's fears are often expressed at times when we are tired and unable to cope properly, it is much easier to tell a child that s/he is making it up than it is to investigate the cause. However, when we do take the time to investigate our children's fears, it often saves much time and energy in the long run.

When I was a child I was terrified of going to sleep. Every night when I went into my room to go to bed, I was sure that there was a murderer under the bed and an evil witch in the closet. Even though I would search the whole room, once I got into bed I was sure there was a place I hadn't looked and that I was going to be killed. Nothing seemed to help. My mother would kiss me and tuck me in, and the minute she left the room I would be terrified. Finally, my father started searching the room with me every night. We would look under the bed and through the closet together. He would close and lock my window and shut the curtains. He even looked out the window to reassure me that no one was outside. Then he would tell me that it was OK to go to sleep. I was finally able to sleep better.

Nightlights are useful for many children. It is important to be alert to whether or not the nightlight is bright enough or whether it just casts more shadows and increases the fear. Some children sleep with flashlights under their pillows so that they have easy access to light and can take it with them to the bathroom if they need to. Sleeping with dolls or stuffed animals soothes some children, while others listen to music. Having a pet sleep in a child's room may be comforting, but there are children who fear that the darkness will transform their pets into frightening creatures. Certain pictures, amulets, or symbols may help some children to sleep.

A child who wakes up screaming or crying from a nightmare is a child who needs comforting. Often children will want to be held, will want the lights or the radio turned on, or will want a certain stuffed animal to hold. A good strategy is to ask the child what the dream was about. Just relating the dream and sharing the fear may be helpful. In addition, it is often helpful to rework the dream.

My four-year-old daughter woke up with a nightmare. She said she had dreamt that a monster was chasing her and that she was all alone. I told her that if she had the same dream again, she should dream that I would come and hold her and that her father would chase the monster away. She fell back asleep and slept through the night. When she awoke the next morning, she told the dream again but with the ending we had worked out—with the monster being chased away.

By reworking the dream the child takes control of both the fear and the powerlessness. Having one or more adult allies helps create a feeling of safety. Having an adult take the dream seriously enough to rework it relieves the child of the sense of isolation that is a major component of nightmares. Another strategy that helps children to sleep better is arranging codes or signals that they can use if they get scared. Often children will wake up too scared to cry out or get up. Knowing they can knock on a wall, blow a whistle, or make a certain sound that will bring an adult is very comforting. This is also a good crime-prevention strategy, as outlined in the previous chapter.

Another common fear is being afraid of someone coming in through a window or door. Having a lock on a child's door creates a fire hazard unless it is a very flimsy lock. However, hanging chimes or bells on the door and on the windows can be helpful. These strategies for handling fear are developed through talking to children about their fears and what they feel they need. A child can be asked, "What would help you go to sleep?" or, "What would help you feel less alone?" The solutions do not have to seem practical to us, as we explained earlier. They will often seem silly or childish or magical. But by taking the fear seriously we are giving our children a very important message. We are letting them know that we respect their reality even if it is not ours. We are also letting them know that we are willing to help them with their feelings. This kind of communication creates the foundation for children being able to tell if someone is abusing them, or for developing concrete and effective safety strategies. Having a nightlight helps a child to sleep, and running away, if they are being followed, helps them avoid being attacked. One strategy deals directly with fear, the other with impending assault. Both strategies help a child feel safer and more confident.

Another useful strategy is to admit our own fears to children. Children often believe that adults are omnipotent and fearless. Telling stories from our own childhoods or about our own lives, including things that scare us, make children feel less alone and less guilty about their fears. It can also be a way of helping children communicate what is bothering them. The following is an example of a discussion we had with a child in one of our classes:

Child: What do you do when you are in the dark and you can't see and you think someone is coming?

Teacher: When I was little I was really afraid of the dark.

Child: Well, what did you do?

Teacher: One thing I did was sleep with a nightlight on.

Child: But my nightlight is too far away, and it's not bright enough.

Teacher: Where is your nightlight?

Child: It's all the way on the other side of my room. My room is really big.

Teacher: Are you alone in the room?

Child: No, my sister is there.

Teacher: Is she younger or older than you?

Child: Younger. She is two years old.

Teacher: Does it help to have her there?

Child: No.

Teacher: What do you think would help you feel safer?

Child: I don't know.
Teacher: Does your mother know that you are scared?
Child: I don't know where she is.
Teacher: Does your mother live with you?
Child: When I get scared in the night, I don't know where she is. She goes out a lot.

The dialogue progressed until we were able to ascertain that this child was on one side of a very large apartment and was left in the care of a housekeeper who didn't speak English. When the child was afraid, she had no way of communicating this to an adult.

Exploring children's fears means taking everything they say with total seriousness and simply asking them for more information. This can be a way to help children sort fantasy from reality as well as helping them to develop coping strategies. The following dialogue took place between a three-year-old boy and his aunt. The aunt had stayed over at the boy's house and had slept in the extra bed in his room.

Child: It was really good to have you sleep in my room because when you're not here the red monster comes in and scares me.
Aunt: Well, we can't let that happen. We'll have to make it hard for him to come in. [The aunt took a big teddy bear and put it on a chair by the child's door]. This bear will chase the monster away. [She then moved a Superman toy to a shelf behind the teddy bear]. In case the monster sneaks by the teddy bear, Superman will get him.
Child: But Aunty, the red monster isn't real.
Aunt: Well, that's good. Now, we don't have to worry about him coming in and scaring you.

By dealing with the monster as if it were real, the aunt helped the child to realize the monster was a fantasy. If the aunt had denied or laughed at the idea of a monster, the child's fear would have remained.

Children also need specific strategies for handling the physical manifestations of fear. It can be explained that heart pounding, shaking knees, butterflies in the stomach, shortness of breath, or an inability to breathe are all ways the body has of saying that it is scared. There are many exercises that both adults and children can practice that help to relieve these symptoms:

DEEP BREATHING

This can be explained in the following way: "When you are feeling like you are getting scared, try to relax your throat and chest. Take a deep breath, inhaling through your nose and exhaling through your mouth. Take the breath as slowly as you can; you can count to five or ten as you do it. Concentrate on your breathing, feel the rhythm of your breathing, and keep this up until you feel less scared."

> When my daughter fell down she got really frightened and started holding her breath in fear. I knew this was bad for her, because I knew that whenever she can't catch her breath, she panics. Then I remembered how it was handled in the self-defense class. So I talked to her very softly and told her, "You are breathing, concentrate on your breathing; you are breathing in and out very slowly." Then I put my hand on her stomach and said, "I can feel you breathing. I can feel the air going in and out. You're doing fine." She started breathing on her own and calmed down and afterward smiled at me and said, "Mommy, we did it."

FANTASIES AND VISUALIZATIONS

Fantasies and the use of images are also helpful in controlling fear. Children naturally fantasize. They can be helped to use their capacity to fantasize as a coping mechanism for dealing with fear. It can be explained as follows: "When you feel scared, imagine something that is peaceful, some place that you'd like to be, people that you'd like to be with. This can help you feel calmer. When you are feeling very weak, imagine that you are really strong. Think of yourself as really powerful. Think of the strongest animal that you know, such as a lion, tiger, or dinosaur. Pretend that you are that animal. Think of your favorite superhero—Superman, Batman, or Wonder Woman. Pretend that is who you are. Think of yourself a really big. Imagine that everyone else is smaller than you are. Feel how strong your muscles are. Take a deep breath and feel all the strength come into your body."

One nine-year-old boy related the following:

> Once when I was walking home from school, I started to feel really scared cause I was on the street by myself. I saw people I didn't know, and I felt alone. So I started thinking nice thoughts. I thought about the things I liked about myself and what I was looking forward to for the rest of the day. I imagined the moon was smiling down at me, and I thought about the nice night I was going to have. I started to feel less scared and got home OK.

PROTECTIVE TALISMANS

Children can carry protective talismans or magical objects. It is helpful to let them choose what the object is that will make them calm and safe. Rings, necklaces, bracelets, small toys, special shirts and sweaters, patches sewn onto jackets, a certain rock or shell, or other small objects can all be empowered by the child to be their magic symbol of safety.

One eight-year-girl who had been sexually assaulted when she was seven carried a tiny toy elephant in her pocket. She described how it helped her deal with fear:

> I always like elephants because they are so big and strong. So I pretend that my little toy is really a magical elephant that can grow up big if somebody tries to hurt me. When I am feeling scared I put my hand in my pocket and I touch my little elephant, and I say to myself, "Nobody is going to hurt me because this elephant will get them."

CHANTS AND SONGS

Having a special sentence, chant, or song when one is frightened can be very helpful. Religious children very often prefer small prayers: "My guardian angel is right here and will protect me." Other children prefer to make up their own: "I am strong

and powerful, no one can scare me." Singing their favorite
song or reciting their favorite tune or poem can be soothing
ways to relieve fear.

One ten-year-old girl related the following:

> I get really scared when my parents go out and I am
> home alone. So I always play the record that has an
> Indonesian lullaby on it. It's a very quiet song, and it
> helps me sleep.

If a child is exhibiting a degree of fear that seems to signal
that something is wrong, there are a variety of ways to help
the child talk about it. Since children often experience their
fear physically, a child can be asked what the fear feels like
or what part of the body it lives in. They can then be asked to
describe what scary feelings look like, what colors they come
in, what shapes they have, what they say, and what they do.
For many children, the fear will take the form of a monster or
shadow. Drawing and playing game are good ways for children
to release fear. The child can be asked to draw the scary feeling
or draw a picture of a time when they were scared. The content
of the pictures can clue an adult in as to what is going on in
the child's mind.

In one case a close friend of a child who had been raped
invented the "rape game." In this game she knocked her friend
down and jumped on top of her. When the children's teacher
saw them playing this game in the schoolyard, the child was
punished. When we explored this game with the child, we
discovered that her friend had been raped on the way home
from school and that this child walked home from school alone.
She was terrified that the same thing would happen to her and
was using the game as a way of controlling her fears.

A sudden behavior change or phobia can also indicate that
something is wrong.

> I was ten years old and walking through the woods.
> I had forgotten that it was hunting season. I stepped on
> a branch and out of nowhere a deer charged. It ran past
> me. Suddenly this man in his red hunting outfit came
> out and started screaming at me that he missed his deer
> because of me. I was so sure that he was going to kill
> me. I kept looking at the shotgun. I was frozen in my
> place, too afraid to run and too scared to cry. I just kept

thinking that no one would ever find me. He continued screaming and then whacked me with the butt of his shotgun. Then he left. I don't know how long I stood there before I went home. I didn't say anything about it, but I didn't go out of the house for the next two weeks, which was the remainder of the hunting season. I refused to wear anything red and kept criticizing my brother or sister anytime they wore red. Finally, my mother figured out it was the color red I was reacting to and asked me why. I just started crying and finally told her what happened. Ever since then I have always wondered about the mentality of someone who would go into the woods and shoot an innocent animal.

When a frightening incident occurs, children need to know the consequences of releasing their fears in order to be able to explain them. Children often feel that if they admit to the fear, the fear will take over, and the incident will take on an overwhelming reality. They try to deny the fear in an attempt to deny the incident. Sometimes they pretend not to be afraid or try not to think about their fears in the hope that they will go away.

When talking to a child about fear, it is crucial to remember how powerful and magical fear feels to children. It is important to explain to children what will happen if they talk about their fears. Children may feel that they will be punished, ridiculed, restricted in some way, or forced to overcome the fear by being made to do whatever it is they are afraid of.

I was fifteen and totally phobic about bugs. I don't know how the fear developed, but I couldn't stand to even look at bugs. My foster mother decided that it was unhealthy to have the fear and that what I really needed to do was understand that bugs are harmless. Unfortunately, the way she decided to communicate that to me was by putting dead bugs in my room. She felt that I wouldn't be frightened as long as they were dead and that I would understand that they were harmless because I was capable of killing them. What happened was I became more intensely afraid of bugs and started checking every room for dead bugs.

As with crime prevention children need to have control over the strategies used to overcome their fears. If they don't feel in control, they are more likely to become engulfed by fear.

For some children the only way to feel in control of fear is by scaring others. The late Alfred Hitchcock explained in an interview a few years before his death that when he was a child his father had played terrifying games with him. He described feeling scared through most of his childhood. As an adult he found that making frightening movies was a way for him to feel in control over the fear. Many adults who witness children scaring other children become angry. It is important to explore with such children why they are putting so much energy into scaring other children as well as to learn what is frightening them.

Sometimes children develop fears and phobias as their way of expressing anger. They may be so frightened of the power of their anger that they transform it into fear. Often this manifests itself in an increasing concern for the person they are angry at. Some children feel that their anger is so powerful it will kill and thus become worried about the person who is the object of their anger. For this reason it is important for children to have positive outlets for their anger so they can sort out the difference between their angry and frightened feelings.

TRANSCENDING FEAR

When we talk to children about their fears and admit to our own fears, particularly in regard to violence and crime, it is important to remember that the fear itself is not going to go away. What we can learn to do is overcome the paralyzing effects of fear, thereby turning the fear into energy that helps us survive. The magic answer to fear is that we are all strong and that fear is part of being human and being alive. We have the power to control our fears.

> The washing machine was being delivered to my house when somehow it fell, and my six-year-old son was pinned beneath it. The delivery men froze. I, who have never been physically strong, picked it up off my child. It was the fear of my child being killed that enabled me to lift it up.

Facing our fears can give us tremendous strength. If we try to get rid of or fight our fears, we can become overwhelmed by hopelessness. If we admit to them and work with them, we can realize that our fears can be useful sources of power and creativity.

Once I started to remember and admit how terrified I was when I was assaulted as a child, I realized that since I had survived that I could probably survive anything. No one could ever scare me again as much as he had. Whenever I found myself scared to do something, I reminded myself how I had survived. I realized that fear did not have to stop me from doing something, that I could accomplish anything I set my mind to do because fear would not be able to stop me. Once I started looking at it that way, I felt much less helpless. Now when I get scared I don't feel as if the fear can take me over anymore. I know it will pass.

Instead of putting a child down for being afraid, we must express appreciation for the child's courage in admitting to and surviving the fear. It takes courage to handle fear. We can treat children's fears as real obstacles. Just as we praise the child who learns to read despite a learning disability, we must support a child who does something they have been afraid to do: "I know you were really afraid to do that. It was very brave of you to do it anyway." The more afraid the child was, the more courage he or she summoned. It is equally important to congratulate children for strategizing and trying to overcome their fears even when they are not successful at it: "I know it was very hard for you to try to do that, and I'm proud that you tried. It doesn't matter that you couldn't get it done; it matters that you tried. That took a lot of courage." Just as children develop creative ways of coping with assaults, so children and adults can develop imaginative strategies for managing their fears. Sharing such strategies helps all of us to be better able to cope with a world that in reality is a very frightening one.

8

Counseling

I was always so careful with my son. I never let him out
of my sight, never let him go anywhere with people I
didn't know and trust. One day when I was walking with
him, holding his hand as we crossed the street, a car
making a turn went out of control and hit him.

We can't promise our children safety. We can't be with
them twenty-four hours a day. Even when we are with them
we can't guarantee that they won't be hurt. We want to believe
that if we are careful enough we can do it; we can protect them
from all harm. When something happens that reminds us that
we can't, we become frightened, confused, and guilt-ridden.
We blame ourselves for not taking enough precautions, for not
foreseeing the dangers. Somehow we failed or this wouldn't
have happened.

After my son and his friend were attacked, I kept
thinking I should have known better than to let them go
to the store by themselves. I should have realized that
two nine-year-olds with money to buy a new baseball
glove would be targeted. Then I remembered that the
money wasn't even taken and that they had gone to the
store by themselves before. It was so confusing. I guess
I expected that I should have had psychic powers. Somehow I should have known this would happen.

We want to believe that it can't happen to our children, that
we will foresee all dangers and protect them. We cling to

everything that helps us to reinforce these ideas. We tell ourselves that our neighborhood or town is safe, that such things don't happen here, and that we are too careful to let our children get into a dangerous situation.

Accepting that we can't promise safety is our first task before we can counsel or be counseled in relation to sexual assault. As long as we believe that no matter what the circumstances the sexual assault could have been prevented, then it becomes our fault if something happens to our child or to children in our care. In addition, we also have to accept our own vulnerability, or we will feel that we failed if we are victimized.

> My children came home from school and found me naked, gagged, and tied to my bed. My daughter covered me with a sheet and took the gag off while my son untied my hands and feet. All I could say to them was, "I'm sorry you have to deal with this." I felt like I had really let them down.

The first reactions of most parents after learning that their child has been sexually assaulted are shock, disbelief, and denial. Because we believe that our children will always be safe, we are overwhelmed when we are confronted with the reality of an assault. We want to believe that it is a nightmare from which we will awake. This is not something our children should have to be dealing with. Many times we'd rather believe that our child is mistaken, lying, or confused. This can't be real.

When we can no longer deny it, we are often immobilized. We don't know what to do, whom to turn to, or where to go. Consequently, we are confused and frightened. Our whole world is turned upside down, our child is looking to us to make things all right, and we haven't the slightest idea of how to begin. Suddenly, we realize that we are helpless. Our minds begin racing as we try to think. We want something concrete to do. At this point parents do a variety of things to cope, including calling the police, going to a hospital, calling friends, or simply holding their child and weeping out of frustration.

> My husband was away on a business trip. I knew something was wrong as soon as my daughter opened the door. She came over to me and said, "Oh, Mommy it was awful," and started to cry. I held her as she told

me that she was attacked by three teenagers. I knew I couldn't reach my husband; I couldn't think of who else to call. I knew that whatever decision I made would be crucial, and I just didn't know what to do. I felt so alone. Finally, I called my best friend. She was a nurse at our local hospital and arranged for us to come in. It was such a relief to have something to do.

Another reaction most parents experience is guilt. Part of that comes from the previously stated idea that if parents are just careful enough, nothing will happen to their child. The other issue, however, is control; if the parents are responsible for the attack, then at least they are in control of it. Now they just have to be more careful and nothing bad will happen again. Parents will often go to great lengths to blame themselves. One mother whose twelve-year-old daughter was raped when an intruder broke into their home while the family slept stated, "It's my fault, really. I used to be a light sleeper when she was a baby. I trained myself to hear any sound and to wake up at the slightest noise that was different. Now that she is older I have gotten lazy." The father in that situation also blamed himself: "She asked for a puppy last year and I wouldn't let her have one. If only I had let her, a dog's barking would have warned us."

Some parents blame each other when they find out their child has been attacked. This is particularly true if they've previously had differences in relation to child rearing. In one situation, each parent blamed the other's restrictions for their daughter's rebelliousness, which led to her sneaking out the night she was attacked.

Another reaction that helps parents feel a sense of control is blaming the victim. If s/he only did this or that, it wouldn't have happened. "If only they had obeyed us" is a common theme. ("Of course it had to happen. I've told her a thousand times not to shortcut through that park.") It's a little harder if the children did all the right things; but we can't deal with our own guilt, so we resort to blaming them. One father of an eight-year-old stated, "She'll have to live with the fact that she didn't resist." Upon further exploration, we discovered he had a great deal of guilt over the fact that he had left her alone in a play area. Oftentimes we have unrealistic expectations of what children can and can't do in a given situation. "I can't believe he submitted. I know they showed him a knife, but he

could have fought. He could have done something," said the
father of an eleven-year-old sexual assault victim. Sometimes
we blame them for simply being children. "How could she
have been so naive as to believe that he was really taking her
into the basement to see newborn kittens?" asked one mother.

A concern of many parents is what others will think of them
as parents if it is learned that their child has been sexually
assaulted. Sometimes this is due to their guilt feelings or because of something someone has said or simply because they
feel ashamed that such a thing could have happened. This
shame may come from their own feelings about sexual issues
or their confusing the sexual assault with sexuality. It also may
come from their sense of having failed as parents in not protecting their children.

> I didn't want people to know my family business, and
> everyone in the neighborhood was asking questions be-
> cause they had seen the police car parked outside our
> home. I hadn't had time to think about what I was going
> to say or how I was going to explain when the questions
> started coming. I felt so ashamed that such a thing could
> touch my family's life. I wanted to move so I wouldn't
> have to keep dealing with the questions.

Having to confront so many uncomfortable and upsetting
feelings as well as our own helplessness often leads to feelings
of rage. Sometimes the rage is at the system that doesn't seem
to really help criminals nor stop their behavior. Sometimes it
is directed at the people who are trying to help because nothing
is making us feel better. Often we want to direct it at the
attacker, but we can't get at him. This may lead to feeling
enraged with everyone and everything because it just has to be
released. Even releasing the rage cannot protect us from an
overwhelming sense of grief. We know our lives have changed,
but we have no idea what the future holds. We know this will
have a lasting impact on our child, but we don't know what it
will be. It feels like a death. Life as we knew it before the
assault will never be the same again.

> I know it sounds crazy, but I felt like someone had
> died and I didn't know who. I kept going into my
> daughter's room and watching her sleep. I kept thinking
> about her whole life from the moment I found out I was

pregnant until now. I kept thinking I almost lost her. I
knew that I had lost part of her, and I wanted it back. I
was like this for months, and nothing anybody said or
did made it easier. It just seemed like something I had
to go through.

The amount of mental energy we expend in trying to deal
with all of the feelings and at the same time support our children
leads to emotional exhaustion. It feels like it is too much, and
we can't do it. We're afraid we will break under the strain.
We begin focusing on how overwhelming it is instead of taking
it one step at a time. It is at this point that we both need and
want outside support.

We are seldom prepared for the reactions of others to the
news that our child has been sexually assaulted. Seeing their
shock and denial gives us a visual image of our own initial
feelings. However, we can't tolerate their asking, "Are you
sure it happened?"; "Couldn't she be exaggerating?"; "He's
always had a great imagination, are you sure he didn't make
it up?"; "She seems fine, how could that have happened?"
When others accept the reality, we are then confronted with
their fears. We are looking to them for support, and they are
telling us how frightened they are for themselves and their
children. If we respond with anger and annoyance, they in turn
respond by apologizing and feeling guilty. They then ask us
what they can do, and we don't know what to tell them.

I don't know what I expected my friend to be able to
do, but I know I never expected her to start telling me
how frightened she was. I was turning to her for support
and found myself having to support her. One day I told
her in annoyance that I needed her to support me and
that it couldn't be the other way around. She started
crying and apologized. Then she asked me what I wanted
her to do. I told her I had no idea, but I wanted her to
make me feel better. She looked as helpless as I felt and
then offered to take me to a movie. I appreciated that
she was trying to do something, and it made me feel less
alone.

No matter how much we love them and how much they
have come through for us in the past, even our friends often
believe the myths about childhood sexual assault. Unfortu-

nately, this means we are often confronted with them blaming us or our child for the assault. We need to keep in mind that believing the myths often functions as a way for them to protect themselves from the reality that this can happen to their child too.

I couldn't believe it when my friend said, "I would never have let my child go to the store by himself. How could you be so careless?" I wanted to say to her, "You are not with your children twenty-four hours a day, how dare you pass judgment!" But I was so shocked, and it played right into my guilt feelings, that I said nothing and just walked away.

Another way that people in our lives protect themselves from the reality is by avoiding us and our children after the assault. Unfortunately, we seldom realize this at the time and feel abandoned when we need them most.

I suddenly realized my best friend hadn't called me in weeks. I called her and asked why I hadn't heard from her. She said she thought I wouldn't want to be talking to anyone right now. I told her that was ridiculous, that I needed her now more than ever. She said, "This is just too much, and if I talk to you, I'll realize how frightened I am." I told her that I was frightened too and that we might be able to work it out together.

When our friends are able to confront their feelings and fears, they too begin to feel enraged. It's not fair that such things happen to children. We should be able to feel safe in our neighborhood. We shouldn't have to feel like we need bodyguards for our children. Such feelings may lead to organized community action efforts.

It was my two best friends who asked for a special PTA meeting after my son was attacked. They were very careful to protect our identities, but they explained to the other parents what had happened and that we needed to strategize as a community in order to have effective safety measures for our children. Within the next week a parents' safety patrol was in effect around the playground.

Often the immediate reaction will vary depending on how the sexual assault is discovered. This may happen in a variety of ways. There may be immediate visual evidence. Someone may see something; for example, a child being taken away by an adult. Someone may find a child immediately after an assault. Someone may walk in while a child is being assaulted. Sometimes sexual assault is discovered in the process of a medical check-up. A child may have VD, an infection, or bleeding. An adolescent girl may be pregnant.

> When the doctor told me my son had gonorrhea I said, "That's impossible, he's only nine years old. How could a nine-year-old get gonorrhea? You have made a mistake." When he suggested sexual assault I said, "But those things don't happen to boys." He explained that they did and then told me that he had been assaulted when he was a child. I guess I have learned a lot since then.

In some cases, a child tells directly what has happened. However, they often give clues before they are able to tell. They may show a new toy that they got for keeping a secret or for being in a special club. They may talk about something awful that happened to someone they know. Or they may make statements or ask questions that seem confusing or disturbing. Some examples are: "Did you know the elevator can get stuck by pushing a button?"; "Mr. Jones said I could be a model"; "Grandpa told me that I'm his special girl"; "Uncle Jimmy told me he would teach me how to be a man"; "There was a man in our house today." Sometimes a child is unable to begin verbally and will display signs and symptoms to let us know that something is wrong.

The most common sign is a radical behavior change. This may take the form of acting-out behavior or suddenly becoming a model child. Children may develop phobias, eating or sleeping disturbances, or unexplained illnesses. They may have frequent crying spells or become accident-prone. Some children begin taking baths excessively or refuse to wash at all. It is not uncommon for a child to suddenly become obsessed with talk related to sexual matters or for adolescent girls to frequently ask questions regarding pregnancy. Running away, depression, suicidal thoughts, and self-mutilation are all reactions of children who have been sexually assaulted but are unable to tell.

I knew something was wrong because I suddenly had
a different child in my house. He was the opposite of
everything he had ever been. He refused to do all the
things he used to do without a hassle and offered to do
things I would never have dreamed of asking him to do.
I thought it was his age; he was eleven, and I knew that
children act out at that age. I never imagined such a thing
could have happened.

As we have stated earlier, there are many reasons why
children don't, or feel they can't, tell that they have been
sexually assaulted. Because sex is a taboo subject in many
families, children may assume that sexual abuse is something
they are not allowed to talk about.

My father once got furious when I described something as looking like a woman's breast. He told me he
would not allow such talk in our home. When I was
assaulted, I was sure he would be furious if I told him
what happened. So I never said anything, and he still
doesn't know.

Some children try to pretend that the assault never happened.
They try to block it out, hoping that if they pretend it didn't
happen, it won't be real. Somehow talking about it would make
it a reality. Other children want to protect their parents from
the pain and won't tell so as not to hurt them.

Every time I try to talk about it, my mommy cries.
It makes me feel really bad. I really have to talk about
it because I can't keep all those feelings down inside me.
But I hate it when my mommy cries, so I don't talk about
it too much.

Some children feel stupid for having allowed the assault to
happen. They feel they should have known better or handled
the situation differently. They don't tell so that they don't have
to deal with others thinking less of them. Some children feel
guilty for having accepted rewards, gifts, favors, or material
goods from the offender. They feel that because they accepted
such items they are responsible for the abuse. They don't tell
because of their fear of punishment or abandonment when others
find out. Many children report self-doubt for having trusted

the offender. This is particularly true if they previously had a close and loving relationship with the offender. Often, children simply don't have the words to tell what happened to them.

> I was only six years old, and we were eating Christmas dinner. I had gone upstairs to my room to get one of my dolls. My uncle came in and said that I was getting to be quite a little woman and that he could help me to be a special woman. He told me that it was an extra-special game and that if I told anybody they would be jealous and would hate me. Then he shut the door. When I came downstairs later, I knew I was different. I couldn't understand why everybody didn't realize it. I asked my mother if she thought I was different, and she said no. Then I asked her if she thought I was special, and she said, "Of course." When I started crying, she couldn't figure out what was the matter, and I didn't know how to tell her.

In Chapter Five, we covered how to help children talk about the problem. The most important thing to remember is that if a child's behavior seems inappropriate to what they are saying, it is imperative to explore further. The environment must remain safe for talking. Opening statements can include: "You seem upset, it's okay to tell me about it"; "No matter what's bothering you, I'll listen"; "I won't be angry. Let's talk about it." Options can be offered: "Tell me as much as you feel you can"; "Do you want to talk to someone else about it?"; "Would it be easier to draw pictures of what is bothering you?"; "You can tell me a story or act out your problem." If these things are not working, admit to your child that you don't know what would help and ask them for ideas.

> I had tried everything I could think of, and she still wouldn't tell me what happened. Finally, I said, "I don't know what else to do. What would make it easier for you to tell me?" She told me she could tell me if I didn't look at her, but she wanted me nearby. So I turned my back, and she told me what happened.

Another useful technique is to use magic. We have used it in several ways. We've picked up a common object, such as a pen, and pretended it was a magic wand. We then instruct

the child to help us make a list of wishes or to wave away all
the feelings that make it hard to talk. After the list is made,
we talk about each item. One of the children we were working
with wished that his father's hands and feet would fall off.
When we asked him about it, he explained, "If his hands and
feet fall off, he won't be able to hit and kick me anymore."
Until that time we hadn't realized how severely he was being
abused. When we had previously asked him about his father's
behavior, he had said that there was no problem.

In other situations we have had the child draw a magic wand
and keep an ongoing list of wishes. Each week we go over the
list to see what changes there are. We've also helped children
create magical planets and beings. An eight-year-old boy, who
was tied to the bed while his mother was assaulted, created a
new superhero who stopped men from doing bad things and
gave children protective crystals to climb inside of when they
were scared. Another child created a magic room that only she
could get inside of. It had a special door that she could open
when she wanted to talk. It was invisible, and she could get
into it at any time. After three sessions she opened the door
and let us talk with her. As we have stated in Chapter Two,
children respond to magic because the world seems so magical
to them. We have found that our willingness to enter their
world helps them allow us in.

Talking about sexual assault is particularly difficult for adolescents. Often they are dealing with breaking away from their
families and becoming independent. They may have been
breaking a rule at the time the assault occurred. They are often
afraid that disclosure of the assault will be used against them.
For example, one fourteen-year-old girl complained that if she
told her parents they would never let her out of their sight
again. It is normal for adolescents to be in a state of conflict
with their parents as part of their development process. Consequently, it is particularly difficult for them to deal with giving
their parents information that may be used against them, or
having to feel dependent on their parents again. Many times,
in their effort to be "adult" in handling their problems, they
don't ask for help for fear that others will think they are being
childlike. In addition, sexual issues pervade the lives of most
adolescents. They often fear that they deserved the assault
because they dressed provocatively, experimented sexually, or

had rape fantasies at one time or another. Other times, particularly if the assault involved an acquaintance, they may not be sure that they were assaulted.

> I couldn't believe he asked me to go out on a date. I had had a crush on him for months. I bought a new dress, perfume, and wore make-up for the first time. When he tried to kiss me, I said no, even though I really wanted him to. When he kissed me anyway, I kissed him back. Then he started touching me. It felt like things were going too fast, and I was really scared. I said no, but he kept going. I started crying and said, "please stop." He just kept going. I think it was rape. I guess I never should have kissed him back. That happened when I was fourteen, and I have never trusted my judgment or males ever since.

When counseling adolescents, it is crucial to acknowledge that they have the right to say yes to some behaviors and no to others. In other words, if they have agreed to kiss someone, that person does not have the right to force them to do anything else.

Many adolescents do not disclose that they were assaulted because they fear their peers' reactions. Sometimes they fear that they will be stigmatized. Many adolescent girls who have been assaulted have told us they are afraid that people will think they are "sluts" if they find out they have been raped. Many adolescent boys fear they will be labeled "cowards" or "unmanly." In addition, adolescents are confronted by misconceptions about homosexuality. Girls fear that the assault will make them lesbian, or happened as punishment for lesbian thoughts and feelings. Boys fear that they will become gay because they were assaulted or that the assailant sensed their homosexual thoughts and feelings. Adolescent boys assaulted by older women fear that they must be homosexual if they didn't respond to her sexually. As stated earlier, it is crucial to explain that sexual assault is an act of power and violence. While an assault may have sexual repercussions, it does not determine sexual identity.

> I was on my way home from a party when I was jumped by four men. I thought they wanted to rob me.

I told them that I didn't have that much money and that they could have what I had. One of them started laughing and said, "No, Pretty Boy, we want you." I tried to run, but I wasn't fast enough. Then I tried to fight, but there were four of them and even though I was fifteen, I was pretty small. I couldn't tell anyone afterwards, because the only thing that kept going through my head was that everyone would keep calling me "Pretty Boy."

Seeking help after a sexual assault may be delayed for weeks, months, or years after its occurrence. Children who tried to tell but weren't heard, weren't believed, or were blamed, will often carry the burden alone until they find an adult who will give them support in dealing with the aftermath. Some children wait until the offender is no longer a threat. For example, one child disclosed incest after her parents were separated, and another disclosed a molestation after the offender was killed in a car accident. Some children disclose in an effort to protect other children from the assailant. We have found that often there is disclosure after a public-education program about sexual assault. This seems to be in response to the realization that they are not alone and it is not their fault. After one of our safety workshops at a local school, a mother called us to say that her child had told her that she was being followed and sexually harassed for over a year. Her daughter related that until she heard us speak she hadn't realized that it wasn't her fault or that she had a right to stop it. The mother told us that she was glad it was finally out because it explained a lot of the problems she had been having with her daughter.

Children who are already in therapy for other reasons will disclose to their therapist if the environment feels safe and they sense that their therapist can handle the information. If, during the initial interview, a therapist simply adds to his or her history-taking the question, "Does anyone ever touch you when you don't want them to?" it will alert the child that the therapist is aware of and concerned about such problems.

One pediatric social worker related the following:

After your workshop I decided to try asking that question, or something similar, for a month. I was amazed at the results. I had so many more victims of sexual abuse than I expected. Some of the children I had been seeing for a while disclosed during that time. I don't know if it was that my awareness increased and I was more alert in looking for it or what—all I know is I had a lot more in that month, and I have had more ever since. Before then I always thought you could identify child-abuse victims by bruises and patterns of neglect. I never expected to find out that basically well-cared-for and beautiful children were also victims of abuse.

Children who have shouldered the burden alone for a while may find themselves overwhelmed by their feelings in regard to the assault. Keeping the secret becomes unbearable and interferes with their lives. Often the secret explodes in the midst of an angry or tearful interchange:

> I don't even remember what we were arguing about when she suddenly screamed, "You don't understand, Daddy. You never will! I couldn't even tell you when I was raped." I was shocked. I didn't know what she was talking about. I waited until things calmed down, and then I went into her room and asked her to explain. She told me she had been raped two years earlier. I still can't believe it. I've always prided myself on being an open and available parent. How could she have been dealing with this for so long? How could I have not known?

Most families have a difficult time dealing with disclosure of a sexual assault that happened a long time ago. It is hard to cope with the thought of a child carrying such a burden alone. We are tempted to believe that they have made it up or that it couldn't have been that bad because, after all, they didn't try to get help. Often we feel guilty. We should have realized. We should have done something. Somehow we should have known. Many families report that past problems suddenly make sense, which often invokes feelings of helplessness and betrayal. What else happened that I don't know about? Is our relationship a lie? What about the other children in my life? What would our relationship have been like had s/he been able to tell? Often this leads to feelings of being overwhelmed, which give way to anger. What is s/he telling me now?

My father sexually abused me from the time I was seven until I was fifteen. The only reason he stopped was because he and my mother separated. After several months, when I was sure he wasn't coming back, I finally told my mother. She said, "That can't be true. I would have known, and you wouldn't be doing so well in school." I pointed out all the problems I had had over the years. She then said, "Well, if it is true, why are you telling me now? What can I do about it, now? Why didn't you stop him, didn't you know it was wrong?" Sometimes I wish I never told her.

Another mother confronted with the same situation handled it in the following way:

I wanted to scream. "Don't tell me, I don't want to know about this." But I could see that it was taking every ounce of her strength to keep talking. She was shaking and kept averting her eyes. I told her it was OK to look at me, that I loved her, and that I knew it wasn't her fault. Then I told her I was sorry she hadn't told me sooner and that I was upset that she'd held it inside her for so long. That's when she started crying. I held her and said, "I know that this has been really hard for you. I'm not sure what I should do next, but I will find out." Those few days are very foggy in my mind, but by the end of the week we found an excellent therapist who'd worked with other families, and we went into therapy together.

The counseling environment must have a safe, supportive atmosphere. Children need to have a sense of control over what is happening and what is going to happen. Rules in regard to confidentiality and information that is shared with parents or other authorities should be spelled out clearly in the beginning. Children should be allowed to have control over whether or not their parents will be present during the sessions. They should be told what is going to happen and why, in their own language. (The specific medical and legal processes will be gone over in the next chapter.) Parents must be sure that the therapist or counselor is willing to go at the child's pace. It is important that both the parents and the counselor clarify to the child that the assault is not their fault, even if they were breaking some familial rules at the time, that they are not bad, even though something bad has happened to them. It is important to remember that the younger the child, the more likely the assailant is a close and trusted person in the child's life.

The physical environment should be child-oriented, with readily available toys, art supplies, and games. The counselor or therapist must be willing to allow the child to just play as well as talk about things unrelated to the assault for the entire session or for several sessions. The child is trying to recuperate from an experience where someone took complete control. It is crucial to the healing process that the child have complete control in the counseling session. Options can be offered in terms of what will be done during the time spent together. In our work, we begin by showing the child the physical environment, giving him or her their own drawing folder, and asking them if they understand why they have been brought to us. The following is an example:

Counselor: Did your mom explain why she brought you here?

Child: She said you would help me with my bad feelings.

Counselor: Did she tell you how or what we were going to do?

Child: She told me to do what you said and then I wouldn't feel so bad.

Counselor: What do you want to do?

Child: I don't know what I am supposed to do.

Counselor: It may be helpful if I tell you about who I am and the kinds of work I do with other children. Then you can decide how you think we should work together.

In this manner it is communicated to the child that s/he is an active participant in the healing process. For the child who has been forced into therapy by a concerned parent, we recommend approaching it as a problem to be solved together. For example: "I didn't know your mom was making you come here. Why do you think she is doing that? Maybe we can talk a little bit and figure out a way to help her understand your feelings. Is there anything that will make it easier for you to be here?" Oftentimes, children are surprised that the therapist can be an ally. They've usually braced themselves to deal with another "problem adult." Finding someone who is concerned about their feelings and asking their advice as to how to proceed often engages them in the therapeutic process.

Children should not have to be in the position of being the only support for their parents. It is important that support systems be set up immediately for parents, siblings, and anyone else in the child's life who is affected by the assault. Home visits are often the easiest way for a child to feel safe with a therapist/counselor. It also sets the tone for parents to be willing to accept outside help. During an initial visit, we recommend that parents and children be seen together and that the counselor/therapist explain that they deserve and need help, that they don't have to go through this alone, and that they are not the only family dealing with this problem. It is helpful to outline for them common feelings and reactions of other children and families.

In a situation involving a twelve-year-old girl who was raped in her building by an unknown assailant, we arranged the interview at her home with her parents:

Counselor: I thought it was a good idea to meet at your house because I know that safety is a very important issue for you right now and that it is hard to feel safe in a strange office with a woman you don't know. I also know that a lot of issues are coming up for you right now that you may or may not want to talk about. I won't press for details. We can talk about them whenever you are ready. I don't know if it will be easier for you if I talk more about my experience working with other girls and their families or if you just ask me questions. Why don't you tell me what makes you feel more comfortable?

Child: How long does it take other girls to get over it?

Counselor: It depends on a lot of things. I really can't give you a time frame. I can tell you that it's good you were able to tell somebody right away and that it is good that you and your family are getting help together. A lot of the other girls I work with felt alone and unable to tell anybody.

Mother: You mean kids really deal with this by themselves? I guess we are doing something right if she told us.

Counselor: It is an indication that you have a strong relationship. That is something that can be built upon in the healing process.

Child: What are other reactions that girls have? Do they have nightmares? Because I have been having a lot of nightmares.

Counselor: Nightmares are very common. What you are

going through is similar to a grief reaction. Just about any reaction is normal. Most girls tell me that they are in a state of shock. They can't believe what happened. It feels like a nightmare, and they are waiting to wake up. After the initial shock wears off, many tell me they feel helpless and over-whelmed. They don't know what to do or how they are going to get through this. Some blame themselves or feel ashamed or guilty. Sometimes they worry about what other people will think. Many times they go over the situation wondering if there was something they could have done.

Child: That is a lot of what I have been feeling. I'm glad you told me. I thought I was a little crazy.

Explaining the reactions of other children and their families serves two purposes: It helps the family understand the range of feelings and at the same time helps them feel less alone.

It must be remembered that the child may be frightened of something the assailant said. It is necessary to clarify with the child that assailants lie and often say things to intimidate people. It is also important to take the child's fears seriously and to help him or her plan strategies that will enable him or her to feel safer. For example, one eight-year-old was told by her assailant that he would come back at night while her family was sleeping and that no one would hear or see him come in. He threatened that he would kill her if she told. She had trouble sleeping, and when she did sleep, she had nightmares. We took her shopping to buy a nightlight and several chimes and bells to put on doors and windows so that noise would be made if anyone tried to sneak in. The child's sleep disturbances ceased after this.

If you feel that the child is anxious to release feelings but seems unable to, there are a number of strategies that can be employed. Asking them to write letters to other children who have had the same experience, telling them about other children, or allowing them to read other children's testimonies can be very helpful. For example, we told a child about another little girl we were counseling. We told her, "She seems so sad and nothing we do seems to help. We don't know what to tell her. What do you think would help; what do you think we should say?" The child responded, "Tell her she is not the only one; tell her about me. Tell her it is not her fault." At this point we were able to explore this child's feelings of isolation and guilt.

When counseling the other people in the child's life who are affected by the assault, it is helpful to remember that they are trying to cope with the realization that the child could have been killed. They are also coping with their own feelings in relation to sexual assault. In addition, they may be dealing with feelings about a sexual assault in their own past that may or may not have been disclosed. Often they are feeling helpless and need to know what they can do to help the child. Outlining common reactions and feelings that others in their situations have experienced is helpful. We often will tell parents what they can say or do to relieve their child's fears as well as how to help with other feelings. In one instance, we had to explain to a family that giving the child special treatment produced more anxiety because it reinforced feelings that he was different since the assault. In another situation, we explained to a guidance counselor that the child's expression of sad feelings during a class meeting was a positive sign, as it was the first time she nad allowed such feelings out.

In our work with a family after incest was disclosed, we explained to the mother that she was not responsible for her husband's behavior, that no matter what she had said or done, *he* had made the decision to molest his children. She could not force him to do that. We explained that we didn't believe that she should have to be a policewoman in her own home. She started crying and told us that we were the first people since this had come out who hadn't blamed her. Shortly afterward, she told her husband, who was an alcoholic, that he could not return home until he was sober and in therapy. She entered a family-therapy program with her children. The last time we heard from them, they were doing well.

In a case involving an eight-year-old who was raped on her way home from school, we visited her class to talk to the children about their fears. We also set up several individual sessions with close friends of the child who was attacked. All the children had a sense of working together to help her recover and to help themselves deal with their fears and feelings about what had happened. In a case involving the friends of a six-year-old who was abducted from her front yard and is still missing, we offered a combination of counseling and self-defense training. We offered this to both the children and their parents because the parents reported finding themselves being overprotective and instilling fear and anxiety in their children.

Often children are secondary victims of sexual assault on an adult. As outlined in Chapter Four, when discussing patterns of attack, there are some attackers who will force children to witness the sexual assault of their mothers or who will use the child as a weapon against the mother. Children who have endured this have special needs. Often this is the first time they realize that their mothers are not all-powerful. Such an experience leaves them bereft of any sense of safety and security. The most secure person in their lives is vulnerable and can be physically and emotionally removed from the role of protector.

Reaction of children in these situations are similar to those of children whose mothers have died. As one six-year-old we were counseling put it, "She is not the same mommy anymore. That mommy will never come back." Many children feel angry at their mothers for not fighting and at their fathers for not coming home in time to rescue them. As one little boy stated, "Mommy didn't even try to fight him. He wasn't that big. And Daddy could have come home early if he wanted to." Other children feel guilt that they didn't know what to do and couldn't protect their mothers themselves. As one child who was aware of adults' vulnerability said, "Children should take self-defense so they can learn to protect their mothers."

As we have stated earlier, it is common for children to develop physical symptoms in response to fear, stress, and anxiety. Consequently, physical working out can be therapeutic. Self-defense adds a sense of power and control, particularly when children are trying to recover from feelings of powerlessness and loss of control. As one adolescent girl said, "Self-defense made me realize that it was OK to let him do that because I came out alive. I also know that if anything else happens, I'll have more options."

When dealing with the issue of how children cope and recover from an assault on themselves or a loved one, it is important to remember that children expect safety and adult protection. The experience of being assaulted or seeing someone they love assaulted leaves them with terror at the realization that the world is not always safe, some adults cannot be trusted, and the trustworthy ones are not always strong enough to protect them. Another factor is that children have very little understanding of the future. They live in the present and vaguely understand the recent past. Consequently, when a child is in an assault situation s/he has no concept that it will ever end.

It may be helpful to point out to the child that although it doesn't feel that way, the assault is over. It is also important to point out to the adults in the child's life that each time the child is fearful s/he will reexperience the terror of not knowing when it will end.

Children are resilient and creative when it comes to coping with sexual assault and the symptoms developed afterward. Some will put their energies into certain areas they excel in, such as school or sports. Others will try to block or forget the experience, perhaps by pretending it was a nightmare or a scary movie. We have also noted that some children will identify with strong celebrities and attempt to model themselves after them. Many children play games, develop fantasies, or tell stories that somehow right the wrong. All of these can and should be incorporated into the healing process. The following is an example of how a child used the combination of counseling and self-defense training in her recovery process: Six months after she was followed home from school and raped, she made up a game where all the children at SAFE pretended to be walking home from school. An instructor was to unexpectedly grab one child. All the other children were to intervene by hitting and yelling until the instructor let the child go. This game became known as the Intervention Game and has since been incorporated into all our programs. This child later reenacted her assault in a counseling session and pointed out all the options she would now have to defend herself if confronted with the same situation. On the second anniversary of her attack, she stated, "It was one half hour, and I am not going to let it ruin my life."

9

What to Do if It Happens— A Step-by-Step Guide

> She stood there naked, bleeding, and shivering. I never
> felt so helpless in my life. I had no idea what to do or
> what to say. I kept thinking, If only my wife were here,
> she would know how to handle this. I knew she needed
> medical treatment to stop the bleeding, but I didn't know
> where to go or what to expect when I got there. She
> looked at me, waiting for me to make it better, and I
> didn't know how to begin.
>
> —Father of an eight-year-old girl
> who was raped at a beach resort

This chapter is written for anyone who may encounter a
child after a sexual assault. We will particularly emphasize
what parents and guardians can do, as they are often the first
contact a child has after a sexual assault and because their
reactions often determine the course of the child's healing process. We will be providing a step-by-step guide to the medical
and legal procedures. We will go over what the child is entitled
to as well as what the child is in need of. In addition, we will
discuss who can help and how they can help.

As we stated in the previous chapter, there are various ways
in which a child discloses sexual assault. Sometimes there is
immediate visual evidence. Some children disclose verbally.
There are situations during which it is discovered—either medically, when the child is treated for other things, or when
someone follows up on the child's display of symptoms. The
disclosure experience for the child is often very frightening.
S/he doesn't know what to expect, often feels out of control,

135

may be waiting for retaliation, and may fear blame or disbelief. In addition, many children are guilt-ridden, either about their own participation or at exposing the offender. Some children also feel guilty because they perceive their disclosure as creating "family problems."

This is a very crucial time for the child. It is important that adults understand what the child needs to hear and be reassured of. First and foremost, the child must understand that s/he is not at fault. It can be explained that bad things happen to good people and that good people sometimes do bad things. No matter what the child did, s/he is not responsible. The adult had control of the situation. At this point, the parent or guardian must reassure the child that no matter what happened, they still love him or her and that they are glad the child told. It is often helpful and relieving for both the parent and the child if the parent acknowledges sorrow at the child's hurt.

Children also need to be reassured that they are believed. Sometimes what they are saying seems incredible or the adult feels the child is lying or the child seems to keep changing the story. It is particularly important to continue to believe them. If they are lying about this type of situation, there is a reason why. It is also an indication that there is definitely a need to look into the matter. The child may be covering up for the offender. It is our experience that children do not claim to have been sexually assaulted when they haven't been. They will change details for a variety of reasons; for example, they will state that the offender was a stranger when it was actually a trusted loved one who assaulted them. As one nurse told us:

> She was brought in unconscious and bleeding profusely. She was only ten years old, and her body was covered with bruises. The internal injuries took hours to repair. When she finally came to, she told the story about a man in a red and white car who snatched her off the street on her way home from school. We brought the detectives in, and she repeated the story to them, but this time it sounded a little bit different. Each time she told it, details changed. I knew something was wrong. Finally, after two days, I told her that I believed her, that I knew she had been very badly hurt, but that I felt there was something she was afraid to tell. I added that it was OK to tell because we weren't going to let anyone hurt her now. She started to cry and said, "But he'll hurt my

mommy." I answered, "We won't let him, it's OK to tell us." Then she explained that there wasn't any man in a red and white car but that it had been her uncle who had threatened to kill her mother if she ever told.

It is also important to remember, as we stated in Chapter Two, that a child's reality is very easily altered. Oftentimes what seems to be a lie to an adult is, in fact, a child repeating a manipulated reality. As one police officer told us:

> She reported that she was let out of school early and that it was Wednesday. She added that it was someone who looked just like her neighbor but that it wasn't him. She told us all about the assault in exact detail, and the medical evidence matched that part of the story. But the school was not let out early, and it was Tuesday. She was eight years old, so she should have known the days of the week. The DA felt we couldn't take the case, so we never arrested the guy. Her mother called me a week later and told me that her daughter had explained that the assailant had gone over the story with her several times. He had insisted to her that it was Wednesday and that she arrived at her house at two P.M. because she had gotten out of school early. It had taken a week for her to sort out that he had been wrong and she had been right. Unfortunately, it was too late to do anything about it legally.

One of the most difficult areas for parents and in fact for most adults is admitting when we don't know what to do. In the aftermath of a sexual assault it is crucial to admit this as the child will pick up that something is wrong and assume that they shouldn't have told. Saying that you don't know what to do and letting them know that you are going to try to find out can be very comforting. It is also important to explain to the child what is happening and why, where you are going, whom you are calling, and what other steps you are taking. The child needs to know that s/he deserves help and that you're going to try to get it. It is also important for them to be reassured that you will stay with them through this process or that you will make sure they are not alone. Explaining that this has happened to other children and that they won't always feel this badly can be relieving as well.

I thought that my whole world had gone crazy and that everything was falling apart. My mother couldn't stop crying; my father was silent. The police officer kept rushing in and out, and nobody was talking directly to me. Finally, a woman detective came in and asked me if I knew what was happening and why. She explained that they would be taking me to the hospital to make sure I was OK and to collect evidence. She also explained that my parents' reactions were quite normal and that I was doing well under the circumstances. She told me that she had worked with a lot of girls who had similar problems and although I didn't believe it now I would get over this; it wouldn't hurt as much as it was hurting now. She told me she would give me names and numbers of people to call so that I could get help afterwards and so that my parents could get help too. That was the first time I didn't feel totally alone.

Stating all the above makes it easier for the child to be prepared to accept help later. It is important for them to know that it is all right to talk about the assault and that there will be people around to listen to them when they need to talk. They also need to know that if it bothers them later on, that doesn't mean they are crazy. It is part of the process. It is an indication that they need help. Getting help should be presented as something positive, not as a sign of their weakness.

I couldn't stand that a year later it was still bothering me. I felt like I was being a baby and that I should be over this by now. My parents didn't know what to do with me, and I was alienating all of my friends. I was even thinking of suicide. Finally, my mother talked to somebody who called me. She said that she knew it was hard but that it took more strength to accept help and face my problems than to continue what I was doing. She then asked what would make it easier for me. She seemed to be really concerned about what I needed and wanted, so I made the appointment.

If the sexual assault has not been discovered medically, it is important to get medical care and treatment for the child. All bruises, cuts, and lacerations should be evaluated and treated.

A general body inspection will note other areas that the child may not be aware of as being physically hurt. Every orifice that has been penetrated should be examined for redness, cuts, objects, and semen. Children should be tested for venereal disease and treated prophylactically. Should the cultures come back positive, there will of course be need for further treatment. The treating physician should fill out a report of a suspected sexual assault and collect the necessary evidence. Most private physicians as well as medical personnel in hospitals are required to report sexual assaults on children to the authorities, if the parents haven't already done so.

The decision about whether to go to a hospital or to a private doctor is a difficult one to make in a crisis. If the private doctor is affiliated with a hospital and can treat the child there, the controversy is not an issue. However, the choice is often between the child being treated privately in the doctor's office or in the hospital emergency room. A private doctor known to the child can be a reassuring figure offering personalized care. In the doctor's office the child is less likely to encounter other crisis situations or long waiting periods. It is important to note, however, that hospital emergency rooms are equipped with everything necessary to perform the required medical and legal procedures. It is also more likely that the emergency room staff has handled other cases and is used to dealing with the police and the legal system. We feel that the decision of whether to go to a private doctor or an emergency room should be the parents'. However, in many cases, parents who initially went to their private doctors were sent by them to the emergency room.

Medical procedures are frightening and upsetting experiences for children, particularly when they have been sexually assaulted. In order to make this process as easy as possible, it is important to remember the child's perspective. Ask the doctor or nurse to explain to you and the child what is going to happen and why. Make sure the child understands in her or his own language. Let the child ask questions. Find out if you are allowed to stay through the exam, and if you are not, ask who in addition to the doctor will be there. Ask that person to spend some time with your child before the exam. The most common reasons that parents and guardians aren't allowed to be with children during exams are that it is against hospital protocol or that the staff feels the child will not fully disclose the details in order to protect their parents (either because the offender is known to the family or because the child fears the parents' reactions). Some hospitals have specially trained personnel to deal with this, who are sensitive to the needs of children and their families at such times. Some hospitals don't allow parents in during the interview process but permit them to be with the child through the examination. You can find out your hospital's policy by placing a call to the hospital administration.

Pelvic and anal exams are extremely uncomfortable under the best of circumstances. After a sexual assault, they are unbearable. Unfortunately, few medical schools offer training to adequately prepare pediatricians and gynecologists for giving these exams to children. In fact, few medical schools even mention the problem of childhood sexual assault, much less the treatment needs of the victims. It has only been in the last few years that medical students have been trained to do pelvics on real people. In the past, and even today in many schools, students are trained through films and the use of mannequins. Needless to say, this training does not prepare future doctors for the reality of examining an injured person, particularly an assaulted child.

Remembering the child's perspective throughout this process is essential. Children do not understand that something will feel "uncomfortable." As far as children are concerned, something hurts or it doesn't hurt. It hurts a lot or it hurts a little bit. For this reason, it is important to tell the child that the examination is going to hurt, that you hope it will not hurt too much, and that it is OK for them to cry if they need to. It is also important to remember that for the child the world has gone crazy and is completely out of control. Therefore the child needs safety and a sense of control. Few doctors are prepared to allow their patients to have control during examinations. This is particularly true for doctors treating children, as few adults are comfortable with children having control over their environment. It is crucial for the child to feel that s/he can stop the exam if it becomes too painful or too frightening. This must be ascertained and agreed to by the doctor prior to the beginning of the examination. It must be impressed upon the doctor that refusing to allow the child such control is experienced as an additional assault.

My mother told the doctor how scared I was and made him promise to stop if I asked him to. He said of course he would. I was terrified. He didn't even warn me when he put the cold speculum in. I let out a yell and he said, "Come on, be a big girl, it will be over soon." I started to cry and I said, "Please stop, this is too much." He got annoyed and said, "It will be over before you know it, just stay still." I looked at the nurse and pleaded with her to make him stop. Then I told him, "You promised my mother you'd stop." I started screaming for my mother, and he yelled at me to stop it and stay still. I couldn't get up. I could hardly move because my legs were in those stupid things. Finally, I told him that he was worse than the rapist. He told me to watch my attitude and reminded me that I was going to be getting penicillin shots. That was ten years ago, and I've never gone for a pelvic exam again.

The above statement was made by a twenty-four-year-old woman who was raped at age fourteen.

Another issue that needs to be addressed is that of the use of general anesthesia. Of the relatively few doctors who are trained to deal with children who have been sexually assaulted, most have been taught that giving the child general anesthesia is better for the child and makes the examination easier. We disagree. It is our experience that general anesthesia further intensifies the sense of loss of control. In addition, it may instill in the child a fear of going to sleep. Many women have reported to us that when they were sexually assaulted as children and given general anesthesia, they awoke in pain, unaware of what had happened while they were sleeping. All of these women have sleep disturbances. If it is determined that general anesthesia is necessary, it is important to explain to the child what is going to happen while s/he sleeps. It is also important to let them know that they will probably hurt when they wake up. In our experience, local anesthesia and a sensitive medical staff is all that is needed in the majority of situations.

Most parents and professionals are at a loss for words when it comes to explaining a pelvic or anal exam to a child. Simple words, analogies, and allowing the child to ask questions can make this a fairly easy process. The following is an explanation that was used by a nurse: "You've been hurt, and the doctor wants to make sure everything is OK. You are going to be checked all over your body for any bruises or cuts. The doctor is also going to check in the places that this man put his penis. That means that the doctor is going to check your vagina and your mouth. This is probably going to be very scary, and it will hurt a bit. It's OK for you to cry, and I'll stay with you. It will be really scary when you first see all the medical instruments. You know how it is when you go to the dentist. All those things that the dentist has look really scary, but they don't usually hurt that much. They are used to check to make sure your teeth and mouth are OK. Well, this doctor has instruments too. They also look very scary, but they usually don't hurt too much either. They are going to be used to make sure that your vagina and mouth are OK. We will talk with the doctor so that if it gets too scary you can say stop, and we'll stop until you're ready to go again. We are also going to ask the doctor to tell you what is happening as it is going on, so that you won't be scared. Do you have any questions so far?"

Child: Is the doctor a man or a woman?

Nurse: We really don't know yet. We've just called for a doctor, and we will see who is coming. Does it matter to you?

Child: I think it would be easier if it was a woman. I feel scared of men right now.

Nurse: It's normal to feel that way. We will make sure the doctor understands how you feel about that, OK?

It is helpful in these situations to ascertain the terminology the child uses to identify his or her body parts. Using words that the child is familiar with will make it easier for the child to understand what is happening.

We feel it is also important to note that warming the speculum is a humane touch that too few doctors recognize. For this reason, we suggest that parents make it a point to request that it be done. It is equally important to emphasize that the smallest size speculum be used when examining a child. This may seem like common sense. Unfortunately, we have spoken to too many nurses who have told us that the doctor used the speculum that was available rather than waiting for or requesting a smaller one. Guidelines similar to the ones discussed above can be used when explaining the anal exam to a child.

It is important to note that with both types of examinations, the child is often in the same physical position s/he was in when assaulted.

> When the doctor started probing my anus, all I could think of was it felt exactly the same as when the attacker did it. I was ready to cry but fighting back the tears because boys are not supposed to cry. I wanted him to stop, but I was afraid if I tried to talk I would start crying. So I held my breath and gritted my teeth until it was over.

Since most hospitals give prophylactic antibiotics after sexual assaults, it is important to prepare the child for injections. Injections are usually painful and often frightening. Again, letting the child know that it is all right to scream or cry and explaining why the injection is necessary will alleviate much of the tension and trauma.

For girls who have already menstruated or who are close to the time that they're expected to begin, it is important to be alert to the possibility of pregnancy. We do not think that anyone should be given DES (the morning-after pill) as it is a very dangerous drug whose risks outweigh any benefits. It is important to note that the recommended dosage for sexual assault victims is 836,000 times the amount that was banned in cattle feed as unfit for human consumption. It is the same amount of estrogen that is contained in a four-and-a-half year supply of birth control pills. This is not something that should be given to an adolescent girl after a sexual assault. In addition, many girls are "DES daughters." (Girls whose mothers were given DES during pregnancy and who may have or may develop numerous medical problems as a result.) Their families may be unaware of this, and the effect of giving a DES daughter a large dose of DES after a sexual assault is unknown.

The risk of pregnancy is small if the assault was a single incident. However, if the girl was gang-raped or repeatedly assaulted over a period of time, the risk increases. There are other medications available, the long-term effects of which have not been tested. Some experts recommend menstrual extraction before it is known if a pregnancy has occurred. Others feel it is better to wait to see if there is a pregnancy and then have an early abortion. This is an unacceptable option for those whose beliefs are antiabortion. Unfortunately, at this time there is no safe medication that will prevent pregnancy after a sexual assault.

There are some people who believe that if a pregnancy occurs it should be carried to term regardless of the circumstances surrounding the conception. In our experience, no one is ever sure how they will handle a pregnancy as a result of a sexual assault of a child until they are confronted with it. We have known girls who have delivered babies who were fathered by their fathers or by their rapists and have given them up for adoption. We also have known girls who have had their babies and kept them. And we have known girls who have had abortions legally as well as those who have had them illegally. In all of these cases, the girls felt that control of their bodies had once again been taken away by the pregnancy, whether it was terminated or not.

Reactions to such pregnancies have included:

"There is a monster growing inside of me. He put a monster in my body" (sixteen-year-old raped by a stranger).

"This is the only good thing that has come out of this situation. I am going to get the chance to give a child life. It is God's way of compensating me for surviving that horrible thing" (eighteen-year-old raped by a stranger).

"I can't wait to get it out. I can't stand that we can't do it sooner. I am afraid that it is going to wreck my insides and that when I want a baby I won't be able to have one. He said that I was his. This was the way he made sure of it" (fifteen-year-old incest victim).

"I was raped by my father when I was ten. I became pregnant and carried the baby to term. I gave it up for adoption. That was nine years ago. I still wonder where my child is and what happened to him. I often have nightmares that he is being burned alive in a fire" (nineteen-year-old incest victim).

Parents of girls in such situations also cannot predict their own reactions. Some parents approach the pregnancy as a problem to be solved together. Some parents are opposed to their daughter's choice, and it becomes an issue they battle over. Other parents are shocked by their daughter's choice, as it is so unexpected. Some examples of reactions of parents we have counseled are:

"We dreaded the thought that she would get pregnant from this. She was only fourteen at the time. As soon as we got the positive test results, we arranged for counseling appointments. We discussed it with several close friends and our minister. It was a painful and difficult decision. We felt she was just too young and decided to arrange for an abortion" (father of a fourteen-year-old rape victim).

"I am a God-fearing woman. There's a reason why God sent this child to my daughter. I have explained this to her. It is just not for her to decide. She'll have the baby, and I will raise it as my own" (mother of a thirteen-year-old gang-rape victim).

"It was bad enough finding out that my husband had a sexual relationship with our daughter; but finding out that she was pregnant was too much. It made me face the issue. When I noticed her putting on weight, I thought it was her body changes because of adolescence. When I realized that she must be pregnant, I wondered who the boy was. When I confronted her she told me, and I went into a state of shock. She was too far along, so she had the baby and gave it up. My husband and I broke up, and now my daughter and I are trying to put our lives back together" (mother of a sixteen-year-old incest victim).

"I have always been opposed to abortion. Then this happened. I was making arrangements for my daughter to have one when she said, 'But, Mommy, you always told me it was wrong.' I can't believe that she would even consider bearing her rapist's child. What have I done?" (mother of a thirteen-year-old raped by a stranger).

In addition to pregnancy, there are other medical reasons why children should be given follow-up medical appointments. Venereal disease may not be detected for two to six weeks despite prophylaxis. In addition, there are other infections that may not be detected immediately. Most hospitals have some form of counseling or social service. Consequently, at follow-up medical appointments an assessment as to the counseling needs of the child and family can be made.

As we stated earlier, most hospitals and physicians are required to report sexual abuse of children to the authorities. The options in relation to reporting to the police vary depending on state laws. In some states, it is possible to report the crime but not prosecute, while in others that is not an option. You can check with your congressional representative or police precinct as to what your options are.

Some parents are sure they want to report the incident whether or not the assailant is known to the child. They view it as a way of getting justice and as a way of preventing future assaults on their child and other children. Other parents know immediately that they don't want to report. They may be distrustful of the police due to a previous experience, or they may simply want to protect their child from what they perceive as further trauma. In some cases, parents do not wish to report the crime because they want to protect the offender or because they fear retaliation. In addition, there are parents who choose to handle the situation privately in the form of a confrontation with the offender or by moving from the neighborhood. There are also cases where the offender is known to the child and the parents confront him and insist that he get treatment for his problem.

In our experience, many children and their families have gotten excellent care from police personnel. However, we have known many others who were treated poorly. In order to prepare the child for the police interview, it is important to understand the components. Police officers need to be alone with the child when they conduct the interview. This is because of the possibility that the child may protect the parent or guardian from certain information, such as the identity of the assailant, the fact that they disobeyed a rule, or the details of the acts that occurred. Parents have the right to ask for a woman officer but must realize that there are not many women police officers and that they will not necessarily get one just because they have requested one. Parents have the right to know what is happening and what will happen so that they can explain it to their child. Many parents tell their child where they will be while the child is being interviewed. They will also remain within hearing distance should the child cry out for Mommy or Daddy. This can be very reassuring for the child if it is explained before s/he goes into the interview room.

Many police officers and detectives have received special training in interviewing children after they have been sexually assaulted. Some use anatomically correct dolls to help the child explain what happened. Often, prior to the interview, the police officer will ask parents what words the child uses to describe private parts. This is important so that the child will not be confused if s/he is not familiar with such terms as penis and vagina. It is important to note that police personnel are focused on the details of the assault. How the assault occurred, what happened during the assault, a clear and complete description of the offender, and where the assault took place are all areas that will be explored during the interview. Police will also ask questions in regard to clothing, description of the premises, and other people in the area. Children should be told that these questions are being asked in an attempt to help catch the offender and not because the police officers don't believe them or doubt their story.

> Calling the police seemed like an important, reassuring thing to do. My friend made the call for us. When they arrived they were so tall, and they had guns and billy clubs. I don't know what I expected, but suddenly I was frightened, and I could see that my son was also. I reassured him that they were here to help us, but he was frightened into silence. Thank God one police officer picked up on how scared he was. He squatted down next to him, spoke to him softly, and said he was really sorry that he was scared. He added that he knew something bad had happened but that if they worked together they could get the man who did it.

When the offender is a stranger, after the initial police investigation the case is usually assigned to detectives for further investigation. The facts of the case are compared to similar cases in order to narrow down the number of possible suspects. Whether or not the offender is apprehended, this process is a very difficult one for the child and the family. It is often confusing and frustrating. Few of us are familiar with the legal process, and each step seems to be part of an endless bureau-cratic maze. Many parents complain that they have to deal with new people constantly. Some communities have streamlined this process by having specialized staffs within the DA's office.

When the offender is known, there is either an immediate arrest or an immediate decision that there will be no arrest. Often the basis for these decisions is not explained to the child's family, leaving them bewildered as to why there is no justice. The most common reason for not arresting an offender is the DA's assessment that the case cannot be won. This may be due to inconsistencies in the child's story or lack of corrobo-ration.

In the stranger or slight acquaintance situations, when a suspect is found a line-up is arranged by the police. The child must be able to positively identify the suspect from the line-up. It is important to explain to children that they will be able to see the suspect, but he will not be able to see them. It is also important to explain that they may not see him or they may not be sure it is him, and that is OK.

After the child positively identifies the assailant, an arraign-ment is held where the suspect is informed of the charges and bail is set. The child does not have to be present during the arraignment hearing. An interview is arranged with the District Attorney to prepare the child for the Grand Jury hearing and to ascertain the facts of the case. Unfortunately, this process usually involves long waiting periods, missed work and school time, and physical and emotional exhaustion.

The next step is the Grand Jury hearing which involves the child testifying before twenty-two adults as to what happened in detail. Children find this process terrifying as they are not allowed to have anyone with them except the District Attorney, who is usually a stranger they have just met that day or the previous day. In one case we were involved with, we waited with the child prior to her going into the Grand Jury room. We gave her a tiny picture of her mother to hold in her hand and to look at when she was frightened. When she came out of the hearing she related the following: "You are going to think I'm really silly. I did what you said. I looked at my mother's picture so I wouldn't be scared. Then I decided I didn't want to hear what I was saying, so I covered up my ears so I wouldn't have to." In our experience, children are amazingly resilient and will often figure out their own strategies to help them through these upsetting processes.

After the Grand Jury proceeding the District Attorney may elect to offer the defendant the option of plea-bargaining. It is important to note that our court system is overburdened and that plea-bargaining often means saving the child from the trauma of having to testify in court and see the assailant again. However, it also means that the assailant has the option of receiving a reduced sentence, which can range from probation to several years in prison.

If the case goes to trial, the child again has to give testimony but this time in front of the assailant. All of the evidence pertaining to the case is presented: the medical records, police reports, etc. This process can take several days. It involves the child having to relive the experience, family life being disrupted, and the loss of school and work time. It also means that the child will be cross-examined by the assailant's defense attorney, whose goal it is to establish doubt in the minds of the jurors. After the trial is over, the assailant may or may not be convicted, depending on the jury's assessment of the facts of the case. If convicted, a sentencing hearing is scheduled. If not convicted, the assailant is free to leave the courtroom. Sentences vary and include suspended sentences, time served, probation with therapy, or a prison term. The sentence depends on the judge and the previous record of the assailant as well as the state laws. In incest cases, which are usually brought before a family court, the assailant may be remanded to treatment, the family separated, or the child removed from the home because in the opinion of the court s/he is not safe there. Often, other social service agencies are involved such as the Bureau of Child Welfare. Ongoing assessments are made until the child can either be returned home or permanently removed from the home.

The other legal option is civil action. This action can be taken against the offender, the party responsible for the child's welfare at the time of the assault, or the owner of premises where the child was attacked. Some families have sued their landlords for negligence over broken locks or poor security in their buildings. Others have sued schools, hospitals, and other institutions where the child was supposed to be receiving adequate care and supervision. Many of these suits have been won with considerable cash awards.

The legal process is arduous and traumatic. However, inroads are being made throughout the country in various specialized programs. It is to be hoped that soon the system will be more attuned to dealing with child victims of sexual assault and their families.

The following testimonies illustrate the range of feelings and experiences of children who have been through the legal process:

> I felt like Mommy was right, that we had to do it. We had to make sure he wasn't going to hurt any other little girls. I hated it. I had to tell the story over and over and over again to so many people. The day that it was over they let him plead guilty to a lesser charge. He was sentenced to six months. All I kept thinking about after I heard this was that it had taken more than six months already. That meant he was going to be out really soon, and I wasn't really protecting anybody. I kept asking my mother why did I have to go through this. He'd be out before we knew it.

> After I told about my father we went to Family Court. We saw so many people—court officers, social workers, lawyers, and the judge. I'm still not sure how it happened, but the judge said I had to be removed from my parents home and sent me to live with my grandmother in another state. I kept thinking, Why are they sending me away? I didn't do anything wrong. He did this to me. Then I kept thinking that I was a real jerk to have told.

> I had nightmares for months, particularly on the days that I either had to be in court or talk to the DA. I cried a lot too. I kept asking my parents when it was going to end. They told me I didn't have to go through with it if I didn't want to, but I felt like I had to. I just couldn't live with the thought that he would still be out there. When I heard he was sentenced to ten years I was thrilled. My parents took me out to dinner, and we had a great celebration. Now I sleep better.

As we stated earlier, families usually need emotional support to help them through the legal process as well as to deal with the long-term reactions of confronting the sexual abuse of a child. Some communities have little or no services available while others offer a wide range. Generally, rape crisis centers and programs offer short-term care for the child and the family. In other communities, there is only medical follow-up, and families have to seek private therapists for the long-term follow-up. For many families, this is the first time they are dealing with seeking mental-health services. Few know how to begin or what to look for. Factors to consider when assessing services include the cost of care, the sensitivity of the staff and their knowledge of the issues, and the type of care offered. As we explained earlier, few professionals have been trained specifically to deal with the issues related to the care and treatment of sexually assaulted children and their families.

> I don't know what I expected. I was recommended to this therapist by the social worker at the hospital. She said that he had dealt with other families before. I told him about what happened to my daughter and how I was having difficulty handling her sleep disturbances and acting-out behavior. He said it was because of my guilt and that I couldn't deal with the fact that she had probably seduced her attacker. I was shocked and confused. My daughter was pulled into a car and taken to an abandoned building and raped and beaten and left there to die. She wasn't found until the next morning. I decided that he was a lunatic and that I was better off without help.

As the problem of sexual abuse becomes more widespread, many therapeutic training programs have touched on issues of victimization. However, very little, if any, of this information has been from the victim's perspective. Unfortunately, this often results in inadequate or damaging treatment for many victims and their families who seek help from therapists. There are many reasons why therapists are unprepared to deal with these issues. They, like everyone else, have internalized the victim-blaming myths of our society. In addition, since the frequency of sexual assault, particularly in regard to children, is denied by society as a whole, therapists may view the child with suspicion: Did this really happen? Is it a fantasy? Is this family overreacting? What commonly occurs is that the therapist begins to project his or her own myths about sexual assault onto the victim or the family.

A related problem is that because of the lack of training in this area, few therapists have been taught how to recognize or cope with their own feelings of discomfort. This discomfort may come from their own fears and feelings of vulnerability for themselves or their families. They also may remember a sexual assault from their past that may be unresolved, never disclosed, or previously suppressed. Some therapists respond to this by becoming overprotective and controlling of clients, which prevents the clients from regaining control themselves. Some therapists respond by blaming the child or the family for the assault. Other therapists endeavor to minimize the impact the assault had. Many therapists find themselves feeling angry or unable to focus on the child's or the family's feelings in relation to the assault. Therapists may feel guilty about that without understanding that their own feelings are normal responses in relation to the issue and that there are ways to deal with them.

Many people believe that therapists are powerful, omnipotent, and immune to the feelings and fears the rest of the population has. It is important to recognize that therapists are people who have certain skills and training but who have experienced the same socialization that everyone else has. Therefore your intuition and instincts are important factors when selecting a therapist. Therapy is a participatory process.

When considering a therapist for your child or your family, you must meet the therapist yourself. Some therapists will give you a free consultation. Others charge for the initial interview. Be sure to determine this beforehand. Many rape crisis centers, hospitals, and other programs that regularly deal with sexual assault victims have names and numbers of therapists who are experienced in this area. It is a good idea to take at least two names to consult since it would be a good experience, if this is your first time seeking a therapist, to compare their styles as well as what you feel comfortable with. It is also important to remember that if you do not trust the therapist, your child will sense that. Before going for the consultation, make a list of questions that you want to ask. Outline the specific points and concerns that you have. What is their background and training? How often have they dealt with this problem? How flexible are they? Will they see the whole family or just the child? What is the charge? How long do people stay in treatment and at what point are other forms of treatment recommended or necessary? When do they consult with other therapists? What is their usual style in handling children? Under what circumstances do they give advice and/or guidelines to parents? In what setting will they see the child? If it is not the setting they are seeing you in, can you see it first? This is important as many parents can tell if the environment is one that their child will be comfortable in. In addition, many parents explore the therapists' attitudes in relation to acceptable male and female behavior as well as their attitudes toward sexuality. The answers to these questions, and your feelings, should help guide you in your choice.

Many families turn to priests, rabbis, nuns, guidance counselors, or other important figures in their lives. Their personal knowledge of the child, the family, and the community often enables them to make helpful suggestions and referrals. If you are considering entering into a therapeutic relationship with them, the same series of questions outlined earlier can be used to help you. No matter whom you decide to work with to help your child and family through the recovery process, it is crucial to trust your own and your child's instincts. In our experience, intuition in regard to these issues is usually right on target. If you persevere in trusting these instincts, you will succeed in finding the help you and your child need and deserve.

10

Beginning to Heal

I feel very free because now I can look at myself and say, "You're all right." I can talk about it.

The human spirit prevails against all odds. The children and adults we have worked with have shown us that the transition from victim to survivor can be made with the proper intervention. We have included these glimpses of their healing so that you can also witness them weaving the difficult unpleasant events of their pasts into hope for a stronger positive future.

HEALING TOGETHER

This section contains two interviews. The first is with four children aged five to eleven years old, who met as a group to offer each other support in the recovery process. We have included this interview because we were impressed with the children's ability to share their feelings and give emotional support. We hope it will encourage others to begin groups to allow children to heal each other. The children are identified as "A," "B," "C", and "D."

D: Sometimes I dream that my mother and father are missing. I'm scared that something will happen when they're not around.

A: I have nightmares that somebody will steal my mother away. I'm always scared that somebody will get her. Sometimes my dreams seem real.

B: I have dreams that somebody stabbed my mother. I run, but by the time I get help, she's dead.

C: I have a lot of nightmares. I don't like to talk about them.

D: I've been upset and scared a lot lately.

A: If somebody comes behind you and they have a knife, wnat are things you can do?

D: Sometimes you can stomp their foot and scream and run away. Sometimes you have to do what they say.

A: The worst things that happened always happened when we were alone. I think that's why we have those dreams. It's so scary to be alone now.

D: I want to learn all the things you can do to get away. I don't want to be hurt even when I'm alone.

B: I make up stories to make myself feel better. I don't like to think about sad things because there's nobody to talk to about them.

A: When I'm alone, I cry a lot. I get scared it will happen again.

C: I get scared about people coming when my mother is sleeping.

B: I get scared when my mother is late. I'm afraid something bad will happen. I'm afraid to get mad.

D: I get scared on my way home from school. People bother us sometimes.

C: I'm afraid of a man coming in.

A: Sometimes, I'm afraid my scary dreams will be real, that they'll happen.

D: For me it's movies. I'm afraid they can be real, those scary movies.

B: I wish somebody would tell me why everybody is so mean. Why do adults do mean things? My Mom says that's a hard question.

D: It's sad to think about. They hurt people and nobody knows why.

C: It's good to get help. Tell people, "I need help, I need help." You have to yell it sometimes, holler real loud.

A: Yelling is fun because nobody ever lets you yell. People hit you when you yell. Adults should let children yell. We have to yell sometimes.

C: Kids should keep looking until they find adults that help.

B: And adults shouldn't take out their angry feelings on

children, it's not fair. Adults shouldn't abuse children.

A: Police should stop adults that do that.

B: If we could be safe, it would be great. I could go outside. I could take the bus all the way to Timbuktu.

A: I could run in the garden. We could wear bathing suits all the time.

D: We could play all day, anywhere we want.

C: We could trust people. I'd be so happy. We could go anywhere. We could have a cookout.

This second interview is with a child and his guardian. It shows the interaction involved in a situation where sexual abuse was recently disclosed. The child is identified as "C," his guardian as "G."

G: When he finally told me, it was like the missing link. Looking back, all the signs were there. The intimacy problems, the not trusting, the nightmares, the waking up constantly, it was all there.

C: I didn't tell because I thought no one would believe me. Grown-ups don't believe kids so much sometimes.

G: He was in therapy. He had a real good therapist. It wasn't making any sense. Something was missing. When he finally told, it clarified everything. We realized what the problem was. We had been dealing with the symptoms for a long time.

C: I decided to tell because I had kept it inside for three years. I figured it was too much. I just told a month ago. It was time to stop running. I would tell another little boy to expect to feel very upset and to try to get help. I would tell him, "Keep telling people until somebody believes you." I would want to tell my mother never to do it again and to get help. I didn't know what she was doing. I was only six years old. When your mother tells you to do something, you do it.

G: If parents think it is difficult sitting down and educating a child about this ahead of time—it is ten times more difficult after it happens. To start educating them and be dealing with what happened is an incredible strain. The guilt, I should have, I should have known. I didn't feel guilty for letting him go visit her, I felt guilty for not knowing. The worst is the guilt and the denial. The child gets the worst of the denial. It hits so close to home. I'm still intellectualizing it. It is hard for me to get angry at her. I was close to her. I believe she was an incest victim herself. Now she is the attacker, the abuser, but at one time she was the victim who didn't get help like he is getting now. I feel sorry that she is going to have to live with this for the rest of her life. I think she didn't raise him because she was afraid she might do that. She really gave it a try.

C: I would tell her, "It is not nice to take advantage of a kid when he doesn't know any better." I want her to admit it and to say she is sorry. Just one "I'm sorry" is good enough for me. Once I had a dream that she admitted it and we went to court and then we went on a holiday. It was the best dream I ever had. Sometimes the feelings just go on and on. It is not going to pass that easily.

I don't tell my friends cause they would make fun of me. But if someone told me I wouldn't say "that's weird" because I have been through it.

G: A lot of his concerns were: Are they going to arrest her? Now that I have told, does that mean you'll never let me see her again?

C: After it happened, I sat down and talked to myself. I said, "Mommy did this because she is sick, she needs help." First I thought I was being punished for something. Then I thought, "No, Mommy shouldn't have done that. You are not crazy." I tried to forget but my conscience kept kicking up and reminding me.

When I found out things like that happen, I realized it had already happened to me. It is a part of me. It will never leave me. There's a piece of it floating up there in my head. Sometimes I pretend my mind is like the ocean. You put things in and they stay, like the Titanic. Talking about it helped a lot. When it was happening I just thought I had to do this because she was telling me to. She's my mother, she said it was normal. She told me not to tell. She said it was just between her and me.

G: What sparked it was sending him to SAFE. I explained it to him, we talked about SAFE at six P.M., and he told me at ten P.M.

C: The feelings keep coming. It's a part of me that I don't want to have. The most important thing to tell kids is get it out, tell someone. And don't just arrest the people who do it— get them help. The most important thing to tell adults is not to do it, cause taking advantage of kids is not nice. And to tell kids what is happening. A lot of kids don't know. Like my teacher once was telling us about sex. She gave us this book, and it was about cows. COWS!

G: I was so caught up in doing everything right for him that I neglected myself in the process. I am still anxiously awaiting my primal scream. I really need that good cry. You can't make these decisions yourself. I am a single parent, I thought, "What I do right now is going to be crucial." I would have liked someone to help with the decisions, be there in case I fall apart. I needed to know that someone would be there to put me together. There were many decisions to make, questions to answer. I hope he gets a better sense year after year that not all women are like that. My concern is that it will affect him in terms of relationships later on. I want him to reestablish trust. To feel that he has choice now and go through the rest of his life knowing that nothing is without choice. I wish that when I was ten that I had someone working on this stuff with me. I'm going to give him what I didn't get. I feel confident now that we have discussed all this that he could apply what he knows to a stranger, a teacher, a relative. I have told him that even if it comes down to me, if your instincts tell you that you are not comfortable with something I'm doing, you have to call me on that stuff. It really pushes all your buttons when they do. A couple of weeks ago he was sick and I was rubbing his chest and stomach with Vicks. I was really tired. He made a point of letting me know that I went down too far. I had been rubbing for two hours. My first instinct was, "Oh, come on," and my second instinct was, "It's working!" I know that if he can confront me, he's well on his way to being safer than I was when I was a child.

C: If there was a world where nobody hurt children, it'd be like everyday between the two of us. If I never had to be afraid, that would be nice. It would be like living in another world.

THE CHILDREN

The resilience of children continues to inspire us. These are follow-up interviews with some of the children interviewed in Chapter Three.

T.

When I think back, I can't believe it. The rape took up so much of my time then. It's all I thought about. It seems like such a long time ago. My life has really gotten together. It's not that I don't think about it, I do, but it's not the same. It's not everything anymore, it's just one thing. I guess it finally is beginning to feel like it's over. I know I won't forget it, but I won't let it stop me either.

Q.

I know my mother is with God. She's in heaven. She's so happy that I got a new mother and a whole family. I'm happy too. I'm learning how to read. I'm learning self-defense. I'm going to be strong when I'm growed up. And you know what? I think this is going to be my family until I'm one hundred years old!

Z.

I told Mommy that I'm going to be a teacher when I grow up. I'm going to teach all the boys to grow up to be good. I'm going to tell them how I used to be scared to grow up. I'm going to tell them nobody has to be mean, they can make the choice to be good. Mommy says she's proud of me.

I.

My mother and I are doing good now. All the problems are normal, the kind of stuff everybody deals with. The same problems all my friends have. It took a while, but we did it.

W.

I have a lot of new friends and I still have some of my old friends. Sometimes I teach them self-defense. I like it because I know all the things I can do if someone bothers me. I teach them so they can know too. I want them to be safe when they're by themselves or when they're with me. It's good to know we can handle it.

X.

If it hadn't happened, I would probably be able to run better, do a lot of things better. I wouldn't be so paranoid when someone is staring at me. It was embarrassing to talk to the police because it's hard to tell someone who knows what to do if they are attacked that you didn't know what to do. I'm glad I know now. When I grow up I want to be a mounted policewoman. If you are attacked and someone says, "Oh, you poor thing," it is easy to accept, but don't hang around them that much. They're going to feel sorry for you and not really help you. Sometimes you just have to tough up.

An important aspect of the healing process for many people is being able to help others coping with the same experience. We have found that one good way to do that is by writing a letter to someone else in a similar situation. This section contains three such letters: one by a child, one by an adult incest survivor, and one by a parent whose child was assaulted.

To Someone Else:
    You don't have to get it out all at once. You shouldn't feel pressure to talk about it when you don't want to. It is scary. Find somebody to talk to. Somebody who is not in your family. I always thought I had to talk about it with my mother. I didn't want to. I thought I wasn't normal. I thought I was supposed to want to talk to her about it. My mom thought counseling would be a good idea for me. At first, I didn't think so. But it was all piling up. So I said OK. It gets easier. You're not alone, even when you feel it.

Dear Friend:
    I know you are hurting real bad because of what happened to you. The same thing happened to me. It's not your fault. You are not bad. I don't know if the person who did it to you is bad or sick but his actions were definitely not right or appropriate in any way. You didn't deserve it. Nothing can justify it. Please find someone you can trust and who is trained with whom you can talk. Start being good to yourself. Grow as a person. Learn well the terms, "self-nurturing" and "not blaming the victim." This terrible thing is one part of your life but not your whole life. Spend your precious time and energy getting your own life in order. Make something

wonderful out of your life. What we do with our own
life is our greatest creation. Never stop painting your
own picture. Rest and reflect, but don't stop. There's a
beautiful world waiting for you, even if you can't see it
now. Please believe that.

Dear Friend:
    Try to remember that:
    You are a loving, responsible, concerned parent. You
cannot protect your child every minute of every day even
though you would like to. Your child loves and trusts
you very much to have told you about what happened.
When something happens to your child it happens to you
as well. It is normal to feel outrage, invaded, and helpless. A crisis as serious as this touches everyone in the
family. The rapist is disturbed. His motive is the need
to overpower and control someone. Your child did nothing to provoke this attack. Direct your anger against the
rapist (but respect your child's wishes about prosecut-
ing). Your child needs your loving support now more
than ever. You have the right to make sure that anyone
who questions her/him about the crime will be sensitive
and skilled. You and your child do not need to listen to
anyone who hurts you with their lack of understanding.
There are people who do understand and can help you.
You will be more anxious about your child's safety, the
safety of other family members and your own safety for
awhile. This is normal. Be patient with yourself and ask
others to be patient with you. If you can't be fully in
control of your emotions right now, it is all-right. Explain
to your child that you are angry and sad. It is OK if you
care. It is appropriate to grieve. You are not alone. Others
have been through this. You deserve the same love,
understanding and support that your child needs. You do
not have to carry this burden in silence. Reach out to a
counselor or close friend. There is nothing to be ashamed
of or feel guilty about.
    And especially remember that: A good parent helps
his or her child learn independence. A good parent does
not take away the child's independence even when the
child has been hurt. You are a good parent.

11

Where Do We Go from Here?

I have been a guidance counselor for thirty-two years.
Fifteen years ago a student who was unusually bright
and beautiful came into this school; a straight A student.
She was referred to me, however, because her teachers
reported she was experiencing tremendous bouts of
depression. I counseled her for months before she finally
told me that she was being sexually abused by her stepfather. I had no idea of what to do. I didn't know what
agencies, if any, would deal with this type of problem.
I didn't know whom I could call. I did the best I could
trying to help. I was sure I wasn't doing enough. She
had wanted to be a doctor. However, in her last year,
she dropped out of school. About a year later a colleague
of mine saw her on the street—she had become a prostitute. To this day I have nightmares about her. I wake
up and see her face in front of me. I feel sure that if I
had known where to turn, if there had been services out
there that I could have referred her to, that she would
have become the brilliant doctor she should have been.
I will never forget her.

Sexual assault of children is a universal problem. Chances
are every one of us knows an adult who was assaulted as a
child, a child who has been assaulted, or a child who is coping
with the assault of a loved one. This problem not only includes
the assault of individual children but children who are abducted
and forced into prostitution and pornography rings, and the
thousands of missing children whose fates we simply do not

163

know. As Dr. A. Nicholas Groth, author of *Men Who Rape*, stated at a recent conference: "If there was an illness as prevalent as the sexual abuse of children, there would have been a national epidemic declared to deal with it."

A problem as epidemic in proportion as the sexual abuse of children must have tremendous societal repercussions. This problem is not only universal in terms of the numbers of children victimized but is universal in its impact on every aspect of society. Ongoing research is uncovering a high percentage of drug abusers, alcoholics, runaways, sex offenders, juvenile delinquents, prostitutes, and teenage suicides who were the victims of sexual assault in their childhoods. While we certainly cannot prove there is a cause-and-effect relationship, it is clearly statistically significant. We also know that not all victims of childhood sexual abuse respond to the trauma in these ways; however, we cannot deny that some of the effects appear to be connected to many of society's ills.

When we begin to recognize all the different ramifications of this problem and acknowledge its epidemic proportions, we understand that it is crucial for all of us who are concerned to take active steps to help in the prevention and treatment of childhood sexual assault. This chapter is a guide to help you start thinking about the possibilities in your community for such programs.

Each community has different needs, resources, safety problem areas, attitudes, laws, medical procedures, crime-prevention services, and capabilities of dealing with child sexual abuse. The first step in thinking about what an individual or group can do involves assessing the services and agencies already existing in your community that may or may not be dealing with the problem. It is important to identify the agencies that should be responding on some level to this concern. Then begin inquiring about the following: Are they aware that child sexual abuse is a problem? What would they estimate is the incidence nationally and within your own community? Are there statistics for the community? What are the reporting procedures? Which agencies are involved in the reporting process as well as the medical, legal, and recovery processes? What are the patterns of attack specific to this community? Are crime-prevention programs and literature related to child sexual abuse available? What professional education programs are there? What community education programs are there? Is there an interdisciplinary task force involved in assessing the services available in the community? If not, would people be willing to get involved in forming such a group? Are there any self-help groups confronting issues related to this problem?

Agencies targeted for other problems, such as substance-abuse programs and runaway shelters, should be questioned regarding their exploration of the issue. Do they have services to deal with children who are sexual assault victims? Would they be willing to expand their services? Would they institute training programs for their staff on this issue? Do they include questions about childhood sexual assault in their intake interviews?

The answers to these questions will give you an idea of what the challenges are within your community. Among the agencies that must be assessed are the police and hospitals as well as clinics, schools, parents groups, martial-arts schools, women's centers, rape crisis programs, legal and child-care agencies. The next step is to set priorities. Think about what would work, what you would like to do, and what needs to be done. Take into account what connections you already have and where your talents lie. For example, as a member of the local PTA you may want to start school-safety programs, or as a therapist you may want to start setting up professional training programs for your colleagues. There are many options as to how to start. Existing agencies can add to or improve their services. New agencies can be established. Interdisciplinary approaches can be refined, built upon, or created. Self-help programs can be established or enhanced. A task force involving representatives from all the different agencies can be created to monitor and evaluate existing services as well as aid to the establishment of new services. Subcommittees can be created to work on such specific issues as legislative reform, writing of medical protocols, public information, and professional training. For many communities, there is an assumption that improving or expanding services necessitates a large influx of funds. Although all agencies need money to operate, often such programs can be established with conservative budgets. It has been our experience that once childhood sexual assault is viewed as a problem that deserves priority attention, resources and funding become available.

The following examples illustrate a variety of ways different communities have addressed the issue:

In one community, as a result of one family's dissatisfaction with the insensitive treatment their child received, a letter-writing campaign was the method used to pressure the local hospital into establishing a realistic and sensitive treatment program for child sexual abuse victims. The police supported this effort since they were concerned that the case could not be prosecuted because the hospital did not take the evidence correctly. The family, with the assistance of a few close friends, researched the outcome of cases in their community. They were able to enlist the aid of the District Attorney's office as well as local members of Congress, when they discovered that many cases that had passed through that hospital had been dropped due to incorrectly obtained evidence. As a result of the community pressure, the hospital assigned a liaison person to deal with child sexual-assault cases and established an ongoing training program for their staff.

In another community, an eight-year-old member of a girls' afterschool group was raped. The group leader, a concerned mother herself, took this opportunity to enlist parent support for providing safety training for the girls. She contacted a woman's self-defense school and with their assistance wrote a grant proposal to provide self-defense and crime-prevention training for the girls. They received a special award grant and were able to offer the program. In addition to developing safety strategies and learning self-defense techniques, the girls were able to discuss their feelings in regard to one of their friends being assaulted. The program became a model for other youth groups in the area.

In one high school, several female students were raped in the school itself. An antirape group was formed by a concerned group of students and teachers. They initially appealed to the school's administration for assistance. The principal refused to see them. They then organized a protest demonstration and called local TV stations for coverage. Several hundred students and teachers marched to the principal's office followed by TV crews from three stations. Under this pressure, the principal granted them an audience. They demanded school-funded self-defense courses for the girls, since the boys were already being given such training as part of their physical education. They also asked that ID checks be instituted at school entrances. Due to the TV coverage, the girls received community support. A local self-defense instructor and rape crisis counselor were contacted and established programs. Police composites of the attacker were distributed throughout the school and community. There were no other rapes reported at that school.

After several children identified the same man as their molester, their mothers organized a meeting to discuss how to deal with the issue. Due to the laws in their locality, little could be done legally to stop this man. They did not believe in vigilante justice but felt that he had to be stopped. They hoped that a meeting would provide a forum where they could plan effective measures to encourage this man to seek therapeutic help. When he learned that the mothers intended to confront him, he moved out of the community. The mothers reported that although his moving added to their own children's safety, they expect that if he has not received help, he is most likely continuing his behavior in his new community.

As these examples indicate, varying strategies can be employed at community levels to deal with the issue of childhood sexual assault. Many communities have instituted Whistle-Alert and Safe Haven programs. In the Whistle-Alert program, children are given whistles to blow when they are in danger or when they see another child in danger. When the whistle is blown, the nearest adult investigates and calls the necessary authorities. In addition, anyone hearing the whistle also blows a whistle. With several whistles blowing, attackers are often frightened away. As stated in Chapter Six, Safe Haven programs are usually the result of a combined community and police effort. Certain stores, restaurants, and homes are designated by stickers as Safe Havens. In the event of danger, children can run to them, and the adults will shelter them and call for assistance.

We have assisted a number of schools in incorporating prevention information into their curriculums. Some schools have developed afterschool programs to teach self-defense and personal safety. Other schools have organized "Safety Weeks," when a number of local authorities are called in to provide information and set up programs. There have been a number of innovative programs throughout the country for the dissemination of information in regard to child sexual abuse, including children's theater groups, films, and booklets.

Often the initial impetus for community programs is a personal tragedy. When a child in your life has been sexually assaulted, the rage has to be channeled somewhere. The most positive channel for that rage is in developing programs that will prevent such tragedies from touching the lives of other children. Unfortunately, this kind of motivation may become hard to sustain as it is a constant reminder of the assault. In addition, many people in prevention programs find themselves uncovering more incidences of child sexual abuse than they are prepared to deal with. This can result in a sense of futility and emotional exhaustion.

If you are going to undertake the creation of a community project of this nature, it is crucial that you begin developing support systems immediately. Some people find that working in a group with other concerned community members and incorporating social activities is the answer. For others, regular meetings with staff to plan how to handle the most difficult situations seems to alleviate some of the pressure. Both professional and nonprofessional workers need to be careful and set realistic goals and limits. Everyone should make sure that they have personal time. In our experience, people who "burnout" are those whose entire lives are devoted to their work, with no outlets for their frustrations and no time that is theirs alone.

Some of the outlets people have used to deal with this frustration include self-defense in martial-arts training, running, swimming, sports, dancing, and other exercise programs; writing, drawing, music, and other art forms; therapy or other emotional supports; religion, meditation, social events, and friendships that are not work-related. It is crucial to stay in touch with your own feelings in relation to this work. Distancing yourself from your feelings for any sustained period of time or denying the feelings or denying yourself an outlet for the feelings results in burnout. Because this problem can seem so overwhelming, it is important to constantly set realistic goals and reward yourself when they are accomplished. It is easy to remember the failures and hard to remember the successes. Working with victims of childhood sexual abuse means facing a number of setbacks and may mean dealing with children you are powerless to help. It is important to remember that although you cannot rescue each child from their given circumstance, your concern and care may be what will sustain that child until he or she is able to get out of the situation.

For us, one of the most effective ways of countering burn-out is dreaming and fantasizing about the future. This book is the result of one such fantasy. We have many more. We hope that a national hotline for children will be established, which a child can call for information as to where to get help and what the consequences of disclosure will be. For the child unable to report at that time, this hotline would provide a counselor with whom the child could discuss feelings anony-mously. We hope all professional schools will begin incor-porating courses on dealing with this issue and of it ramifications. Given the current statistics, we think it is unconscionable that such courses do not exist.

We would also like to see all martial-arts schools offering realistic, effective, and sensitive programs for children on per-sonal safety. We would hope to see treatment programs for families and offenders developed on a wider scale. We've al-ready seen and hope to see more of children actively partici-pating and supporting each other through the recovery process. We have trained children to help teach self-defense so they can be involved in the prevention aspects as they grow. We think it is crucial for children to act as rolemodels for other children.

We also hope to see more adults intervening on behalf of children on an individual as well as a community basis. If adults would become involved upon witnessing a dangerous situation or when called upon, a safer world for children would result. Other visions of the future and of a safe world are included in the final chapter.

12

Visions of the Future

In order to build a safe future we must have the ability to imagine what it would be like. Children use fantasy and dreams often. As adults, we must remember how to do this. Keeping our visions helps us stay hopeful and gives us ideas for tangible ways to work towards our goals. The following statements and letters by adults and children express their thoughts about how to heal and their visions, both real and fantastical, of a safe world.

Someday, I'll give this to my mother:

Dear Mom: I know you did the best you could. It was all so hard for you. When I was growing up I thought you hated me. I thought you were sorry you had me. When I told you, I thought it proved that I was no good, more trouble than I was worth. I know now that it confused you and scared you. You didn't know what you could or should do. I felt like an orphan. Emotionally, I had no mother. There were other things I never went to you about. Other things I couldn't tell you. I didn't want you to have more reasons to hate me. I was so sure you hated me. I thought I was unlovable. When other people said they loved me, I didn't believe it. You couldn't love me, how could anybody else? I never could trust people who said they loved me.

I finally reached the point where I know that is not true. I know I am loved. I have a lot of love in my life. I finally realize that you love me too. That you loved me then. You couldn't give me what I needed because

171

you didn't know how to, not because you didn't want
to. See, Mom, I've turned out OK. My life is good. I'm
strong and beautiful, and I know how to love myself. I
can trust people now. My world is so much brighter.

Mom, you can hold me now. I won't stiffen or pull
away. You can hold me; I'm still your little girl. Our
tears can wash away all that pain. I forgive you, Mom,
and I love you. Your daughter.

My fifteen-year-old daughter was raped two years
ago. In ten years she will be twenty-five. What would I
like for her? A goal for herself. A way that she can be
satisfied within herself without always needing the val-
idation of others. The ability to experience the unexpected and have adventures rather than being afraid of
loosing her controls. To allow herself to make mistakes
and show vulnerability. To be able to love and trust men,
either as friends or lovers or both. To have been able to
share the information about her rape with someone special who'd be sensitive to the issue. To be orgasmic. To
feel good about going through a major trauma at a young
age and coming through it with some understanding and
feelings of self-worth. To sleep free of nightmares. To
allow herself the gift of intimacy with a special love or
at least be heading in that direction. I hope she will be
able to understand some of why I reacted so weakly at
a time when she needed my strength. I hope she'll
understand and forgive her brother's reaction with its
survivor-guilt complications. I would wish that they can
be close again someday. I want her life to be as good as
it would have been without that goddamned RAPE. To
be comfortable enough to seek counseling if something
is disturbing her. To have the worst trauma of her life
behind her. To be free of the fear of rape . . . but how
could she be, and what woman is? Let's put it this way . . . in
ten years our society will have addressed the problem
and rapists will face severe consequences for their ac-
tions. This will help free survivors and all women.

I hope the space program will discover a planet where
there is no crime. Then we can learn how they did it and
do it here. It would be great, no one would hurt kids
anymore.

I couldn't believe on my tenth anniversary the pain was so deep. It was the essence of sadness. I was mourning for that fourteen-year-old child and what happened to her. And I was saying, "You have a right to this." But I was also saying, "It is over, look what you have learned." I hope that in ten more years I will not be as sad as I am now. I hope I will be past the point I am at now.

I had this piano teacher for years. She watched me grow up. I often thought about calling her and asking her if she noticed anything. When I am ready, I will. I want to know more about what I was like as a child.

In ten years I'd like to look back at it and think, it is there, I can deal with it. It was a struggle. I came out of it all right. I don't want it to come up a lot or be a nuisance. I hope my mother will look at it as something we had to deal with that she no longer has to deal with. It's mine and it's over.

If we could create a safe world for our children, there wouldn't be any victims. It would be a lot freer. Children wouldn't have to be afraid to be affectionate. Parents wouldn't have to be afraid. We would change it so adults saw children. Just because someone is two feet tall doesn't mean they are not a person. We would give adults that awareness. If the world was safe, children would have as many options as anybody. There would be no boundaries, no reason to have so many rules. People could trust each other. There'd be so much less anxiety—it would free up a lot of energy.

If the world was safe for children, I could come home and relax for half an hour without being panicked if my son was five minutes late. There is always that little nagging "what if" that never goes away. It is there 365 days a year. I'd be a much better parent without it.

I want my son to be able to train in the martial arts solely for the sheer beauty and spirit of it, without coping with the fear that he might have to use it in his own defense. If he could do that, he could do everything else.

I want my child to have an emotional bank account, so if anything bad happens to him he'll have something to fall back on. I want him to develop his full potential. If anything happened to my child, I would tell him that before he is a victim, he is a person first. As terrible as it is, it is not his whole life. I would get him the best possible help right away. I would tell my child that even if his behavior is unlovable, *he* is still lovable no matter what.

In ten years, I'd want to feel like I wouldn't have to have someone watching my back to be safe.

I would like one day, twenty-four hours, to not feel frightened and to feel safe. Self-defense training helps a lot. It gave me my sanity. It gives me a way to channel it. I'd like to see all kids get training.

To this day I can hardly ever fall asleep with a man. If I could be safe for twenty-four hours, I would go to the park and lay out a blanket by the water. I'd gather men around me and rest and sleep in their arms.

I think children should learn how to defend themselves in a supportive atmosphere. I think boys should learn to respect the feminine qualities in themselves and therefore respect girls and women more. I think children should be taught from a very young age to appreciate their strength. That would change things.

A safe world? It would be like heaven. Not exactly like heaven but just like God wanted it to be. We could go out and leave our doors unlocked. We wouldn't have to use keys. We wouldn't have to kill or have guns. It would be so great. It would be perfect.

Afterword

How to Evaluate Children's Safety Programs

It is crucial to critically evaluate how we are teaching our children about child abuse. Children deserve a first-rate education about a subject that involves their very lives. When evaluating programs and educational materials, think about the following points:

Respect for children. Too many programs and materials merely give a set of rules for children to follow. A quality program and any materials must contain the child's perspective and understand the child's point of view. It should foster a sense of confidence in children and their abilities. Ask children who have participated in the program or used the materials: What are their opinions? Was it fun or frightening? Do they feel better about themselves, the same, or badly? Children are the best evaluators of children's programs and educational materials. As we noted in Chapter 9, this is also true for aftercare programs. Children know after one or two sessions whether they are being helped. Trust their instincts.

Accurate information. It should be emphasized that children are most often assaulted by someone they know. Assaults often happen in places considered safe (home, school, playground). Child abusers are both men and women, of all racial and ethnic groups and classes, and come from all walks of life.

Defining dangers clearly. The words *sexual abuse, rape,* or *child molesting* should be stated, as should the correct names for body parts. A working definition of all forms of sexual abuse should be included. Definitions of assault, robbery, kidnapping, and physical and emotional abuse are also helpful and important.

Realistic strategies. Children should be taught a series of options for what to do if confronted with abuse. They should learn, for example, what they can do if they try to say no and the adult doesn't listen. Many materials avoid mentioning times when children are faced with violence. Children must have options for those situations. Review the skills and strategies noted in Chapters 6 and 7. Are they included in the program or materials? Are there games and fun activities to help children integrate these skills? The educational process requires practice, the program must include practicing the skills and strategies.

Positive approach. Materials should be presented in a positive and non-threatening manner. Children can be taught self-protection in the same manner in which they are taught how to handle themselves in case of fire and how to cross the street. Children should be told "success stories," where they learn of actual incidences when children escaped assault or got help after something happened.

Disclosure. It must be emphasized that if a child is abused, it is never the fault of the child. Children must be told that cooperation is a viable self-protection strategy and that survival is the right thing. Information should be included explaining to children what they can do if they are abused, as well as their options and what to expect after disclosure.

Presentation of materials. Make sure that children of various racial and ethnic groups are represented. It is also imperative that children from different kinds of family situations are shown. Materials which constantly stress "Go tell mom and dad" are invalidating to children who don't have a mom or dad they can tell, or are in a situation where a parent is being abusive. Materials must also show that girls can be strong, and that it is OK for boys to show feelings such as fear and sadness.

Credentials. Since child safety has become such a "hot" issue, many people who don't have the necessary expertise are jumping on the bandwagon. People conducting programs or writing and producing materials should have training and experience in psychology, social work, or education as well as crime prevention and crime-victim counselling. Find out how long they have been working in the field and make sure that they have had actual experience teaching children prevention and/or working with abused children.

We owe it to our children to tell them the truth about child abuse. They need not be frightened or overwhelmed but rather empowered in their own defense. We can provide them with realistic and positive strategies for survival while fostering a sense of inner safety and strength.

Index

counseling and, 133–34
definition of, 78
in elevators, 88–89
at home, 86–88
introducing adolescents to,
81–83
introducing children to, 78–
81
techniques of, 89–99. *See
photographic insert*
cooperation, 95–96
physical resistance, 96–
99
positions and blows. *See
photographic insert*
yelling, 92–95
Self-esteem, 5
Sexuality, ambivalence about,
43
Shopping, assessing danger
during, 58
Signs and symptoms of sexual
abuse, 54–56, 121–22,
123–24
Songs, 109–12
Spearhand. *See photographic
insert*
Speculum, 142

Ta'ismans, 109
Teasing, 5

Therapy, 151–53
See also Counseling
Touching, right to refuse, 69–
70
Trial, 149

Venereal disease, 145
Visualizations, controlling fear
and, 108–09
Vulnerability
behavior stereotypes and,
44–45, 48
child-rearing and, 7–16
fear of punishment and,
66–67
feelings of powerlessness
and, 48–49
parents' sensitivity and,
47–49
traditional concept of
"goodness" and, 65–66

What-if games, 79–81

Yelling, 92–95
You're So Cute exercise, 13–
14

SAFEKIT for Kids

SAFEKIT is a mini-course in personal safety for children. SAFEKIT is a diverse learning experience that empowers children, in a non-alarmist practical manner, to be safer in the home, at school, on the street, and in stores. This unique kit provides the *first comprehensive safety material, developed from classroom experience, for children of all races, utilizing their own words and images.*

SAFEKIT, featuring a 48-page activity book, 30-minute audio cassette, emergency contact ID tag, "I'm a S.A.F.E. Kid" poster, and colorful stickers, provides immediately effective safety strategies. Combining physical and psychological aspects of self-defense, this unique kit allays children's fears and increases their confidence and protective skills.

Special Offer for *Your Children Should Know* readers: The authors have decided to offer SAFEKIT at a special discount to their readers (regular price: $14.98; readers' price: $6.00)

Order Form

SAFEKIT _____kits @ $6.00 each   Total $_____

Postage & handling: $2.00

   ($1.00 for each additional kit) $_____

Please add local sales tax (if applicable) $_____

                           Grand total $_____

*Make check or money order
payable to:* SAFEKIT

                                 Mail to: SAFEKIT

NAME:_____   Dept. H & R

                                      7 Nowell Farme Rd.

ADDRESS:_____   Carlisle, MA 01741

_____

* No stamps or CODs. Canadian Readers: please use U.S. dollars.

Special Discount Prices Available for Bulk Orders. For Information Send S.A.S.E. to: Electronic Media Associates, 161 West 15th St., New York, N.Y. 10011. Or Phone: (212) 206-0020.